MW01592847

Coming Home

Leaving Busy

To Save My Soul

by Melissa R. Cassidy

Independently published by Melissa R. Cassidy

Melissa@leavingbusy.com

All scripture quotations are taken from the King James Bible.
Cover image by kieferpix from Getty Images Pro via Canva Pro

Caution: The information contained in this book is intended to be *solely* for inspirational purposes. It is assumed that the reader will consider their individual circumstances, get counsel and pray before making life-altering decisions of any kind.

ISBN: 9781688797055

What Readers are Saying

"I just finished going through the whole book. I think it is beautifully written! It was very inspirational to me. It got me thinking about what I can cut out of my life to be more "rested.""

AUBREY KNORR
www.facebook.com/AubreyKnorr.EditorandProofreader/

"I can't begin to tell you how much I enjoyed reading the book as it hit home for me in a lot of places."

LAURIE HANSCOM HARMON
seekingserenityandharmony.com

"I thoroughly enjoyed this read because it perfectly aligns with where I am in my own journey. I could totally relate to your point of view. I think you did a great job covering the spiritual aspect of the lifestyle, even for non-believers. I like that you included questions to reflect on the information covered. Overall, I would give this book 5 stars! Thank you so much for sharing."

MELANIE HARMON
moderndayalice.com

"This book resonated with me on many levels because I am in a mini-life season change. Your words have helped me to refocus my plans and to not allow myself to be distracted by things that could be considered sloth-like throughout the day. My time is more valuable than I have given it credit for."

TANYA SUTER
realisticacres.com

Contents

Part IV: Setting the Record Straight

Part V: The Lost Art of Rest

Part VI: Getting Finances in Order

Part VII: Economy of Happiness

Part VIII: Slowing Down Your Mind

Part IX: A Matter of Health

Part X: Braving Alone

Part XI: Finding Your Tribe

Part XII: Spiritual Perspective

Part XIII: Setting Intentions

Part XIV: Let Transformation Begin

Acknowledgements

Even though I wrote, edited, designed and published this book independently, there were many helping hands along the way. Without the generous time and energy of these special individuals, this work would not landed in your hands looking and reading as it does.

Thank you to Tanya Suter, Aubrey Knorr, Tabitha Grant, Melanie Harmon, Laurie Hanscom Harmon, Catherine Ciaramitaro and Shawn Cassidy for reading my very rough first draft. It was your input and encouragement along with schooling me on all things grammar that brought my writing concept to life.

Thank you, Sheri Ciaramitaro, for advising me on the fonts for my cover design. You were a life-saver!

Thank you to all my wonderful friends and fellow bloggers who cheered me on and voted on my endless cover concepts. I needed help and you delivered.

Dedication

My personal journey of rest, the start of my blog and the writing of this book would not have been possible without the financial and emotional support of my best friend and husband, Shawn Cassidy. Thank you, Shawn, for loving me through life's seasons, investing in my dreams, enduring our budget cutbacks while providing for our needs and listening to me through the entire journey. I love you and I'm grateful to be sharing this adventure with such an understanding man.

Ultimately, I give the glory and honour of writing this book to God, who not only bequeathed me the gift and desire to write, but the experiences and words with which to describe them. It is only through God's unmerited grace and favour that I have anything of any value to say at all. My hope is that all who read will share my gratitude and awe for our creator and designer of all things.

Foreword

Melissa is one of the hardest workers that I know and whatever she puts her hands to, she gives 100%.

This book is a project that she has desired to write for a long time. She understands what it means to feel as though she's spiraling out of control and needing to take a break to re-focus and prioritize her life.

Her thoughtful stories and excellent teaching will resonate with those who feel burnt out, and will assist in helping them to find balance, purpose, and meaning.

Whether you're a young mother, a busy entrepreneur, full time worker or an active volunteer, this is a must-read; especially those struggling and overwhelmed with life's demands.

This book offers practical and spiritual guidance to help regain perspective and control over the many demands you face. Leaving busy to save your soul will do just that!

PASTOR CATHY CIARAMITARO
Co-leader of Open Bible Faith Fellowship of Canada
Founder Windsor Life Centre
(Melissa's mother)

Catherine Ciaramitaro is also the author of:

The Cross

and

101 Reasons to Live a Cross-Centred Life

A Word from Shawn

There is a feeling of peacefulness that comes from slowing down your pace, living on less and not being consumed by the need to buy the latest gadget.

Having Melissa at home and available to help with the day-to-day tasks that need to be done, creates an atmosphere of peace in our lives. This in turn opens us up to being more present in the lives of our friends and families.

When you look back at your life, will you remember the house you lived in, the car you drove, the job you had or will you remember the people that you shared your life with?

I hope this book helps lead to balance and rest to your life.

SHAWN CASSIDY
(Melissa's husband)

Part I: Purpose

Chapter One

Share My Story

The purpose of this book is to share my story of how I came to recognize a deep need for rest and a more sustainable lifestyle; how I found the courage not only to voice that need but to seize an opportunity to fulfil it. Although I have had many life adventures that required specific trainings, I have no formal post secondary education or major achievements to boast of. It's very likely that you, the reader, have more education and professional experience than I do.

I do possess one remarkable skill; I have the ability to take information and put it into practise. Not necessarily in all things at all times, but in enough things at the right time to accomplish an array of interesting goals for someone who hasn't achieved a traditional education.

In our age of information, there are many who know all the right things to do and say. Despite the vast knowledge available at the press of a button, there is a significant lack of ability to put it into **practise** in our lives. Who knew that being teachable, examining oneself and making then executing plans were valuable life-skills? I sure didn't, but it has served me well.

This book is not a result of high intelligence or superior achievement. It is simply my story, a biography of my thoughts, observations, and experiences as I enter the post-child rearing, menopausal season of my life. It is the gift of wisdom I'm extending, not only to my daughter, but to all daughters everywhere.

Chapter Two

Validate and Help Others

t isn't enough to share my story just for its own sake. If you are entertained for a few hours that is good, but this book is meant to be so much more than that.

You need only to listen and you will hear the spoken and unspoken longing for rest that threads conversations.

The question, "How are you?" is often responded to by a sigh and a weary, "Tired" or "Busy".

"We have _____ and _____ going on BUT AFTER THAT we can _____ (insert breathe, sleep, rest, deal with issues, connect with friends, vacation)"

Students juggle studies and work. Young families navigate work while raising children. Career people try to keep it all together as they climb their corporate ladders. Mature people are sandwiched between the needs of their adult children and aging parents while preparing for retirement. Some are living out all of these life stages at once!

The theme is the same even if it morphs with different characters and events.

Some women I speak with feel trapped in cycles of busyness that have been thrust upon them by circumstances, loved ones or employers. Other women choose their fast pace, propelling forward by desire or passion from within.

Whether a woman is being dragged along by life through situations out of her immediate control, or wholeheartedly plunging herself into an active season of frantic activity, they will both need reprieve and refreshment.

Perhaps my words will give voice to the thoughts and longings of women everywhere as they read this collection of personal experiences and summaries.

It is not enough that I find a life of rest and sustainable pace alone, while my sisters struggle to breathe in the ocean of their lives. Perhaps my thoughts and ideas could serve as a life-preserver and an infusion of hope to those who have given up on

rescue to a better place long, long ago.

I feel a moral obligation to humbly say that I could be

completely in error as to my own conclusions in this book. I would

never want someone to make a life altering decision solely on my

arguments in this writing. As with all decisions, the choice to work

less and rest should be made prayerfully and with wisdom.

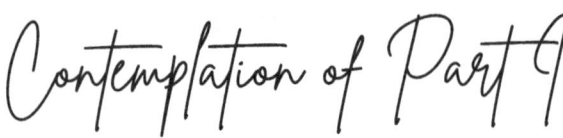

Contemplation of Part 1

1. What motivated your decision to read this book?

2. What life phase are you currently living out?

3. When people ask you how you are doing, does your busy schedule ever become part of the conversation? How?

4. If you feel trapped by busyness, do you feel as though it was thrust upon you by others or is it coming from within yourself?

5. Are there areas of your life where your practise doesn't match up with your knowledge?

6. What would your life look like if it allowed for rest and a pace that was sustainable?

Note

Part II: Introduction

Chapter Three

Setting the Table

am writing this book from an extended season of rest from work called a sabbatical. Since my employment position wasn't conducive to taking a year off and I couldn't guarantee my return afterwards, I decided to resign.

In the 18 months prior to this decision to quit my job, I had been doing a lot of soul searching and practise of spiritual disciplines. This increase in spiritual activity and contemplation was a recognition that I was coming to the end of myself. I was yearning for a deeper connection to God and a need for renewed purpose.

This pre-sabbatical journey started with a 40-day partial fast from food in January 2017. Over the span of my adult years,

I have explored the spiritual discipline of fasting in an effort to refocus on my faith and increase my physical health. Typically, I practised shorter fasts drinking only water for 1-10 days but I had always longed to complete a longer fast. Keenly aware of my physical limitations in the context of work and life demands, I thought it wise to compromise my ideals and complete a modified fast. As a result, I cycled through a variety of self-planned eating and fasting progressions over a six-week period. Oh, how my heart was longing for renewal in my spiritual life!

Embarking on 40 days of dedicated focus on God while alternating between hunger and restrained eating was personally important to me. Many significant events in the Bible occurred in a 40-day time-frame including Moses' wait on the mountain for God's instruction (Deuteronomy 9:11) and Jesus' fast prior to being tempted (Matthew 4:2, Mark 1:13, Luke 4:2). I didn't know what the outcome would be but I sensed a need for change in my life and was eager to move toward it.

Incidentally, the culmination of that fast ended right before a corporate prayer and worship conference at our church called

"Ignite". Lead by Corey Stark and his "Ignite the Nations[1]" team, the conference focused on pairing scripture readings, spontaneous prayer, and live responsive music. I was so inspired by the vibrant approach to prayer that I joined an initiative to learn, teach and practise this prayer technique.

For a season, I attempted to use Sundays as a day of rest which included a 24-hour fast, morning church service and an evening prayer meeting. I became so enthusiastic about prayer and fasting I hosted a couple informal weekend retreats for friends who wanted to practise this together in my home while my family was away. It was a wonderful time where some ladies were introduced to extended fasting for the first time. We have great memories of those intimate gatherings to pray and reflect.

In the autumn of 2017, I participated in the 8-day "Immerse[2]" program at the International House of Prayer (IHOPKC) in Kansas City. The theme focus of the week was

---

[1] Ignite the Nations
http://www.coreystark.com/
[2] IHOP Immerse program:
https://www.ihopkc.org/immerse/

"Building a House of Prayer" which was timely since I was actively involved in our church's initiative to utilize IHOPKC's prayer model.

IHOPKC's Immerse experience involves approximately 20 hours of teaching by the Immerse leaders in line with the week's focus, approximately 20 hours of prayer and reflection in their 24-hour prayer room, and some small group discussions and fellowship. It was an amazing experience!

Upon arrival, I sensed this was a very special place. The very first session began with simple group worship and the moment the music began to play my eyes filled with tears I didn't even know were there. Suddenly, I realized that I was mentally, emotionally, spiritually and physically exhausted and this unique place of ministry felt like a spiritual spa where I could be ministered to.

During the session introductions, the current Immerse leader, Corey Stark, posed the question, "What would you ask God for if you were guaranteed the answer would be yes?" Like most people, I had a list of needs that could be recited, but as I sat reflecting with my pen and paper, all I could write was that I wanted an extended time of rest: a whole year. I still have that written prayer.

It felt impossible and at the time I had no idea that I was setting events into motion with that realization. It was simply what I hungered for most.

When I returned from that week away, I started attending early morning prayer almost daily. It added to my already busy schedule but I felt the time in worshipful reflection was a special place.

In January 2018, I embarked on another 40-day fast yet I was discovering that my fervent prayer and fasting was not yielding the fruit one would expect. Instead of being more patient and content, I was feeling frustrated and angry. There were many emotional outbursts and crises. Reflecting on this now, I can see many reasons for my emotions. I was living out a life direction and pace that was too demanding for me to sustain. Anyone or anything that added to that burden triggered distress. I was a very tired and angry Martha who wanted very much to live a Mary

life. (Luke 10:38-42)

In the midst of that turmoil, I had the privilege of visiting

the Holy Land. It had been a life-long dream. Even this

experience aroused conflicted emotions for me. On one hand, I

felt a deep connection with the physical visiting of places I had

only read about in scripture along with a new appreciation for the

reasoning of conflict in the Middle East. On the other hand, I was

agitated by the hectic pace of the tour and the toll overseas travel

had on my body. I was not rested at all when I returned from

"vacation".

There was much more going on behind the scenes. I was

experiencing burnout, grief and disillusionment. There was an

observation that I was pushing too hard in prayer and worship

and that it would be advisable to pull back.

This wasn't what I wanted to hear. The quiet, worshipful

times were what I clung to and I didn't want them to stop. If

anything, other parts of my life were going to need weaning

instead.

By May, I was ready to leave my job but didn't make the final decision to resign until August. The decision terrified me yet also gave me a glimmer of hope for the future. I stayed in my work role until November so we could find and hire someone qualified to take over my work.

In the meantime, I used my last week of vacation to make the pilgrimage to IHOPKC for a second 8-day Immerse. This time the study focus was "Growing in Prayer and Prophetic". During this visit I was impacted by a movement within IHOPKC's ministry that had begun just prior to my visit. Pastor Mike Bickle, IHOPKC's founder and overseer, was introducing what he called, "The Mary of Bethany Heart Connect" focus. This new focus meant IHOPKC was trimming programs and activities, especially their annual Onething Conference[3], to provide opportunity for their ministry community to slow down, rest and be more relational. It was an acknowledgement that leadership had been

---

[3] Read explanation behind pruning of Onething Conference:
https://www.ihopkc.org/resources/blog/last-onething-conference/

pushing at full force to achieve their great vision — an approach that tended toward using people to the point of burnout. It didn't surprise me that the many ministry endeavours that revolve around their 24-hour prayer room, an oasis of worship and prayer rest for worldwide visitors, had actually become a hub of frantic Martha-like activity for the staff and volunteers who made it happen.

Not only was IHOPKC echoing my own longing to rest and build relationship but my favourite worship leader, Misty Edwards, was not leading any of the worship in the prayer room during my visit due to her own declaration of ministry sabbatical.

It was surreal to be reminded that it was in this sacred place that I had first voiced my desire to take a sabbatical. Only one year later, I was standing at the precipice of what I had assumed would be impossible. I was also experiencing confirmation all around me that this was not my own isolated desire but a movement rippling throughout the body of Christ. It was a joyful week!

This book is a recollection of my tired heart yearning for rest and home, how it became a reality and the preciousness I discovered upon arrival. It is my advice and wisdom to those who feel that the driving pace of life is holding them captive from a place of rest and sustainable living.

I sincerely believe that however challenging and frantic my journey to this place of realization and fulfilment was, that it was birthed from this season of prayer, fasting and reflection.

As with all events that birth change, I can look back and be filled with gratitude for everything that brought me to the place where I now sit writing these words to you. Truly all has come together for good. God has been extraordinarily kind to me.

I'm here to tell you that I believe that if you are hungry for rest and home, that God will be extraordinarily kind to you too.

Chapter Four

Coming Home to Nothing

I am not really sure when my life began its shift. My children were growing up and becoming immersed in their own plans. My discomfort definitely became keener when my daughter left home and went to live in another city a couple hours away to attend university. It was as though gravity had released me from its grasp and I was floating.

I responded the way most people do, I guess. I threw myself into the ever-building list of things that needed to be done at work and invested in the prayer ministry I was a part of at church. We were doing okay financially and had little to hold us back from whatever plans we wanted to do on the weekends.

On the inside, I grew deeply unhappy. I couldn't shake the empty feeling in the pit of my stomach when I came home every day. It felt like after a day of work in a lonely office that I was returning to a house devoid of welcome, warmth and comfort. Even if my husband was on day shift and my son was home, we were like three separate entities not connecting.

I was most often in the kitchen trying to keep up on meal prep, my husband was trying to do household chores and fix our belongings quicker than they could break, and my son was running his mowing business or playing Xbox with his friends. My daughter was busy working, studying and attending classes with little time to connect.

Even if I carved out some time to walk the dogs or relax, I couldn't convince my family to abandon their activities to join me. The reality was, there was work to be done, places to be and things to do. It left me feeling that there was never enough time for true connection. We would often spend our vacations trying to catch up on the chores we weren't getting done during work weeks instead of relaxing and enjoying a rest.

One summer, I had weddings to attend on two consecutive weekends and it sabotaged my work weeks because I didn't get my food prep done on the weekend as I typically do. Scavenging for lunch items and suppers when tired and hungry is no way to live.

Over the years when something needed to happen that no one had the time to manage, I would joke, "We need to get one of those stay-at-home moms". It was my funny way of reminding my family that I wasn't one and couldn't be expected to do all I had done before going to work full time.

This was part of my growing angst with my life. My home NEEDED me and I needed everything to be okay there in order to give myself to anywhere else. Even though I didn't have young children anymore, my home was still screaming out its need for me. In fact, without my children there as an emotional tether, I had no fuel to draw on in my other activities.

My household needed someone to inhabit and manage it properly and consistently. Someone needed to be the person to greet everyone home and help everyone else in and out every day. I was the heart of the home and it felt empty because I wasn't there anymore and no one else had stepped in to fill the void.

Perhaps we are a bit more particular about the quality of our meals or the organization level of our home. Or perhaps I am just more sensitive to the sense of isolation that busy cohabitation fosters. I know people who are more easy-going and others that appear to be more adept at doing it all.

I am confident though, if I sat every one of my friends down and asked them if they could maintain the standard of living they currently enjoy while working less, every one of them would express a desire to slow down, if not leave the workplace altogether.

If leaving the workplace wasn't possible, most everyone would like coming home at the end of the day to a tidy house with a meal simmering on the stove. Having someone there to celebrate your return and inquire about your day so you could unburden yourself and exchange daily experiences with would make a great difference.

Then after a healthful meal with meaningful connection, it would be idyllic to then turn your attention to some necessary home tasks or projects and be done in time to relax with a book before bed. When finally closing your eyes to begin a night with

the proper amount of sleep, you can reflect on a day well spent

and all vital chores being done so that tomorrow will be productive

and successful as well

Chapter Five

Defining Rest

What is rest anyway? You're going to hear this word frequently in this book and it's important for me to bring this word forward so we can examine its meanings. According to Google's Dictionary, rest means to cease work or movement in order to relax, refresh oneself, or recover strength.

Ceasing Work

Work is a complicated word. Most of us immediately think of our employment first and are all too glad to dream of not having to clock in at our jobs. The majority of us exchange our time, energy and skills for money in an agreement with an organization or company of some kind. Most job arrangements have a set number of hours per day and week and a pre-established agreement on statutory holidays and vacation. The entrepreneurial person may not have the same formal arrangements but they often find themselves working at the whims of customer's demands. There are few individuals who are independently wealthy and don't have any responsibilities that go along with the privilege of enjoying financial enrichment.

Work is not only referring to our paid jobs but to our unpaid responsibilities to our community in volunteering. Many people volunteer a degree of their non-employed time to contribute positively to society in some way whether it be in the realms of education, religion, health care, social assistance, politics or other venues. Our avenue of volunteering reflects the values that we hold close to our heart.

Home and family administrating are work as well. Making meals, washing the car, cleaning the house, changing the oil, taxiing children to events, medical visits and such all amount to energy expenditure. In fact, it is very difficult to do anything, even fun things, without a degree of work to prepare and clean up afterwards.

Working out, exercise, is also a form of work. I find it somewhat poetic that as much as we have removed physical movement from most jobs, we still have to ensure that we spend some of our time doing a physical activity to keep our bodies healthy. The most blessed among us either get our physical activity from their jobs or from activities that they truly enjoy. Otherwise, for the rest of us, the time spent exercising can be pure grind.

Even many hobbies, activities that bring us joy and often only emerge after the above tasks are done, involve work. Whether you are refinishing a piece of furniture, tending a flower garden, restoring an antique car, crafting, painting and any other industrious passion...it is a work of love.

Relationships have work involved too!

Work is vital to well-being and survival. It is intermingled in everything we do and in all parts of life so it seems impossible to escape for even a minute, never mind for any significant length of time. However, we should refrain from or minimize work for certain periods in order to accomplish a goal.

Ceasing Movement

Ceasing movement is the kind of rest that many think of when the word is spoken. Sitting or laying either with or without media such as a book, music or television. Sleeping: the average adult needs to cease movement 7-9 hours in a 24-hour period. This allows our bodies to do the internal work that it cannot do while we are active during the day.[4] Deprivation of this time affects our performance, can endanger ourselves and others and even lead to death.

Relaxation

Relaxation is fairly straightforward. You can do a light activity like walking to clear your mind or watch a television program when your body is exhausted from work but you're not ready to go to bed.

Physically, when you sit, your legs get to relax from holding you up. When you lay down your core doesn't have to support you upright. When you close your eyes and fall asleep in

---

[4] Sleep recommendations:
https://www.helpguide.org/articles/sleep/sleep-needs-get-the-sleep-you-need.htm

the dark, you get a reprieve from processing external information, thinking conscious thoughts and movement.

Refreshment

Refreshment is a little more difficult to quantify. Do you remember a time where you felt "refreshed"? It may have been after an amazing sleep, or it may also have been after a great swim or a productive business meeting. Refreshment can be experienced after an encouraging word or a weekend at home checking a few important tasks off a to-do list. What refreshes one may not necessarily refresh someone else. An activity that you find refreshing one day may feel draining the next. Refreshment is more elusive and subjective but it should definitely be a by-product of good rest.

Recover Strength

Hopefully, after a period of rest one would experience the ability to return to their work activities without the exhaustion they felt when their work ceased. If you wake up feeling as poorly as you did when you laid down, something is wrong either with your rest, your body or with the activities that you've been engaged in.

An adjustment in any, or all of those three, may be needed for you to recover properly.

When I speak about resting for a prolonged period, I do not mean days, weeks or months of unadulterated physical relaxation where you lay or sit, do not move or do anything productive. Not only would long term idleness be detrimental to your mind and body, but it likely wouldn't be very interesting or fun and you probably would feel terrible afterwards, not refreshed and recovered of strength.

I had to think about this. What *does* constitute rest in terms of activities?

When comparing a conventional eating approach to the Ketogenic way of eating, you will notice that the pyramid illustrations show a reversal in consumption quantities.

This concept of reversal displays similarly when applied to seasons of work and rest. Employment and high responsibility volunteering need to cease completely during rest periods to provide more time of relaxation and enjoyment.

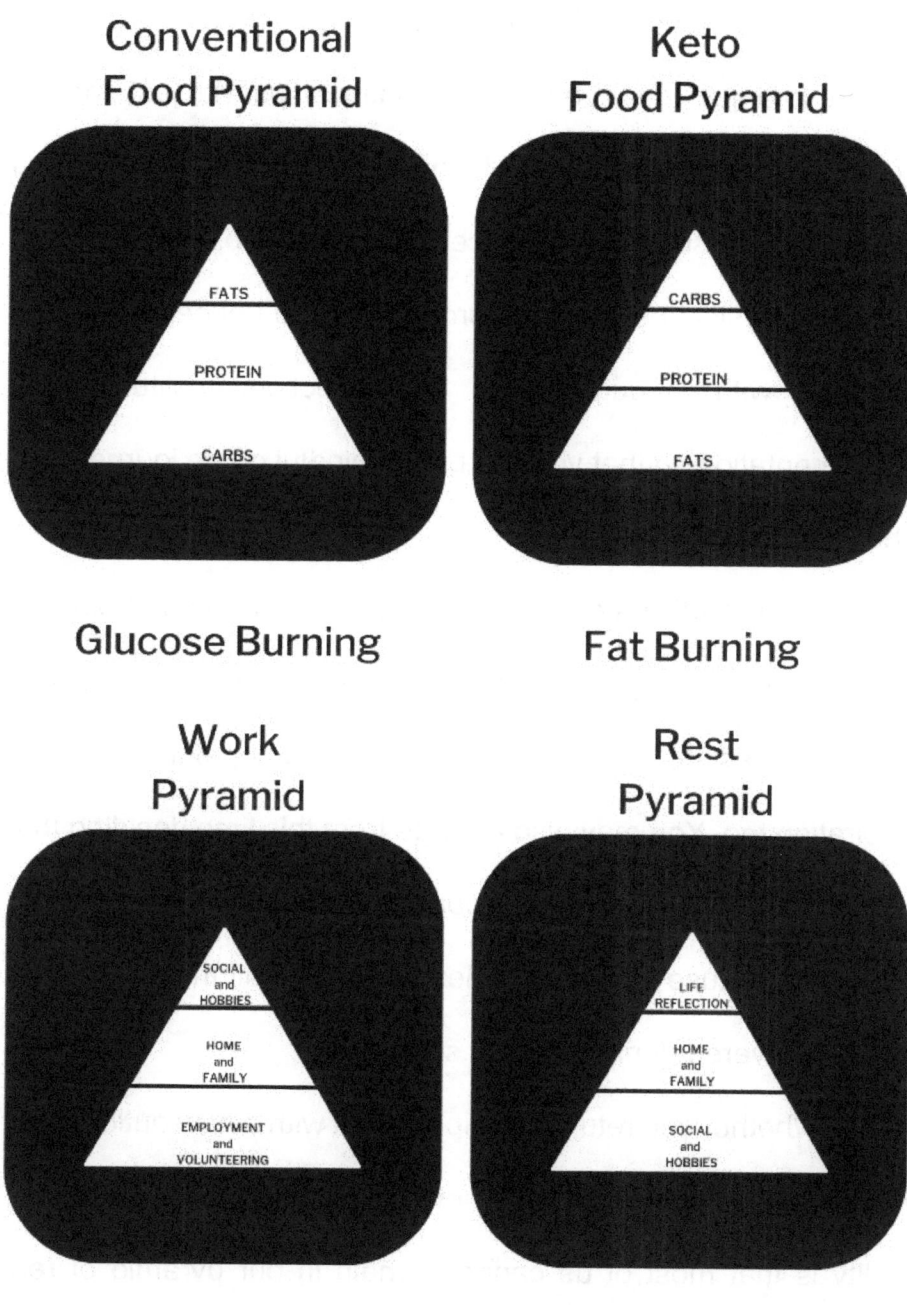

Conventional
Food Pyramid

FATS

PROTEIN

CARBS

Glucose Burning

Keto
Food Pyramid

CARBS

PROTEIN

FATS

Fat Burning

Work
Pyramid

SOCIAL
and
HOBBIES

HOME
and
FAMILY

EMPLOYMENT
and
VOLUNTEERING

Earning

Rest
Pyramid

LIFE
REFLECTION

HOME
and
FAMILY

SOCIAL
and
HOBBIES

Non-Earning

Without your employment and intense volunteer work, you are free to enjoy your hobbies and relationships with just enough exercise and home/family administration to keep everything afloat. Making sure that balance between sleep, relationships, hobbies, physical health and home or vehicle upkeep are taken care of with enough time for reflection, solitude and experimentation so that you are being mindful of the journey and what it is meant to teach you.

If you participate in rest with this mindset, you should be able to return to your employment and volunteer activities relaxed, refreshed and with new perspective...hopefully, with new inspiration too. You may also emerge from this time deciding that you are going to change your employment and volunteer activities because you realize they no longer suit the person you have discovered during the rest season.

Whether you return to employment with a new outlook and life strategy or embark on a new employment adventure, the reality is that most of us cannot remain in our pyramid of rest indefinitely. This can be welcome but it can also be saddening if you really enjoyed your discretionary time allowance. If you find yourself feeling forlorn about the demands on your life that keep you from activities that give you rest and enjoyment, you may be encouraged by some thoughts that inspire me with hope.

As a Christian who reads the Bible, I often see mirrored reflections of spiritual principles in life and nature. Not only do I believe that the practise of balancing work and rest to be God's directive for our life on Earth, but I believe that rest here on Earth points to our after-life in eternity. (Hebrews 4:1-12)

Most people have a conception of heaven that involves us floating around in the clouds at an eternal church service worshipping God. I read a book called "Heaven" by Randy Alcorn that purports (with scriptural references) that heaven will be more than that. We will have new bodies (II Corinthians 5:1-3), homes (John 14:2), work, and rest reflective of what we have here on Earth, but without the corruption that started with Adam, Eve and the forbidden fruit. (Revelations 22:3) There will be differences for sure and heavenly existence will revolve around the worship of God.

Imagine with me what life would be like without corruption, pain, greed and other forms of evil (Revelations 21:4). I believe we will live in a realm that is modelled after our pyramid of rest. Certainly, the gap between work and rest will become less frustrating and difficult. Eternal rest with God in heaven will become something more beautiful and productive than we could ever dream of.

In the meantime, however, we must find a way to balance work and rest in the measure we have been given here as flawed humans in a flawed world.

Chapter Six

Marathon Living

S ince rest must always give way to work, are we destined to live yo-yoing between the two extremes of hectic frustration and indulgent, restful pleasure? It is certainly a reality for most people who live the traditional work and vacation model we follow in North America: the whole go, go, go, relax, go, go, go life rhythm that we don't even question. Even if one is fortunate enough to enjoy a year-long sabbatical, returning to the standard busyness of work is a difficult transition without some adjustments to the pace.

We've all heard the term, "It's a marathon, not a sprint." It's a reminder that going too fast in a long-distance run is counter productive. Unless a runner has trained to a pace, they will likely race too fast at the start only to lose steam part way through. A slower runner who paces themselves will make it to the finish line before those racers, if they even finish at all. Aesop's fable of the "Tortoise and the Hare" in which a slow tortoise wins a race over a speedier, yet overconfident rabbit, has a similar message.

Slowing down doesn't just apply to work here. It applies to spending and certain entertainments as well. If your employment needs are mandated by your financial needs, then reducing your financial needs would serve to reduce your employment needs. The concept of living on less than you earn is foreign to prosperous nations of people who regularly spend MORE than they earn as a whole. Even our governments spend more than they collect! We live wanting more and working more so naturally we are resting less.

Before I move on, I recognize that not everyone is in a position of working purely for excess spending. There are many who are being excellent stewards of their resources but even so, their living situation requires that they must work beyond ideals talked about in this book. My words are not meant to condemn or dishearten you. Instead, I would encourage you to put into practise whatever elements of faith and rest that you are able and trust God to expand your opportunities.

Even those who are able to slow down should do so judiciously. It's not feasible for the masses to leave their jobs and it would be detrimental to society since most organizations and companies provide valuable services to society. We would be in trouble if there was no-one to collect the garbage, fix broken pipes, build homes, do bookkeeping and manage administration work teams. Most every job is vital to society in some positive way. I say *most* because there are a few industries that are less than helpful to society.

What is feasible for many people is to live beneath their means and work a little less. Consider the jobs that would open to unemployed people and the increased satisfaction in the workplace. Rested, creative, inspired workers coming to their jobs with enthusiasm and appreciation knowing that they can afford what they need and will be able to rest again soon. Sounds amazing, right? Idealistic. Yes. That doesn't mean it can't be done.

The point is that no-one is going to make this happen for us. We individually have to look at our lives and decide where we ourselves can make changes and then make them. Everyone's situation is different so the application of rest and work will be varied by circumstances.

If enough people step back from their lives and make the adjustments necessary to their spending and working habits, societal change will happen naturally. There are a few companies setting an example of balance and well-being but those jobs are coveted and rare. The government can get on board by providing incentives and creating awareness.

In the end though, it's best when this balance comes from within ourselves. We have a responsibility to face the challenge of pacing ourselves and not getting caught up in competition. There will always be those who would race out the gate, gobble up as many work hours as possible and show off their achievements, flashy possessions and experiences as a result. As we see the racers running ahead appearing to gain ground leaving us behind feeling like we have lost some cosmic competition, we need to remember our why and stick to our modest pace.

Then when those who went too fast, spent too much and lived too hard hit the wall of exhaustion and consequence, those of us who have paced silently from behind will continue past to finish well. That's why this book isn't just about resting, it's also about learning how to live life in a sustainable way. Slow down, pace yourself, and keep going. That is what sustainable life pace is all about.

Chapter Seven

Significance of Home

I could have written a book purely about rest and living life at a sustainable pace without the emphasis on the value of home, but, for me, it wasn't an option. Home, to me, is the epicentre from which rest, love, and abundance is cultivated and flows out to the world.

In writing this, *I wonder* if my nostalgia for home is not a mainstream concept anymore. *It could be* that people's experience of home is so changed that my romantic notions of its centric comfort and therapeutic benefits are no longer relevant to the newer generations. I can only speak from my perspective and have to include my thoughts and affections for home because it is who I am and what I believe. Home truly is where my heart is and I totally agree with Dorothy from the movie "The Wizard of Oz" that there is "no place like home".

In today's house-flipping market, the sentimental value of abiding in one place by choice for a lifetime is less heard of. Moving from house to house was my childhood experience and it probably had a lot to do with why I was so eager to cultivate roots.

I've been blessed to find a house with my husband that has enough of what we both want to be our forever home. We've lived here for 16 years so far and I often tell friends that we will live here until our kids insist we need to be put in nursing homes. It's a house with an upper level and basement so I add that, when we are too old and feeble to do stairs, we will put those chair lifts in and hire a house-keeper and outdoor help.

No-one knows what the future holds and I do have an adventurous streak in me so this may play out differently than how I now imagine, but the sentiment is there. I love my home. To some it is enviable and to some it is a starter, but to me it is a mix of dreams, sweat, tears and memories that can never be replaced.

As I will describe in later chapters, however, I've learned that home is not so much the house but the ones who inhabit it and in order to inhabit, you must have time to do so.

That is why the topic of rest and home are so intertwined for me. I hope that at the conclusion of this writing you will have a greater appreciation for the special people in your life and the place you gather together every day called home.

Contemplation of Part 99

1. Have you ever heard of a sabbatical before? If so, where?

2. Have you wanted to observe a year of rest? If so, would your current employment allow for that?

3. Have you ever embarked on a spiritual journey that lead to an unforeseen destination? If so, please explain.

4. If you could ask God for one thing knowing the answer would be "yes", what would YOU ask for?

5. Have you experienced an unwelcome shift in your family life? If so, please explain.

6. What is your family life like? If you are busy with separate activities, do you feel connection?

7. Can you identify with Melissa's frustration in managing work, home, and social arenas?

8. Do you ever wish you were free from your work so you could take better care of your home and loved ones?

9. What would an ideal day look like to you?

10. Do you make time for rest and refreshment in your life? What

    does that look like for you?

11. If you are not getting enough time to rest and do activities that

    refresh you, what would you need to do to make that happen?

12. Do you feel like the pace you live your life at is sustainable?

    If not, what does "crashing" look like for you and what are you

    doing to cope?

13. If you made the radical decision to slow down your life to a

    manageable rhythm, what would the fallout be?

14. Do you identify with Melissa's sentiments of home and its

    importance? If so, how do you feel about yours?

Notes

Part III: Challenging Mindsets

Chapter Eight

Getting to the Root

Mindset is everything. Until we understand what is driving us to make the choices that we make, it will be difficult to change, especially for the long term.

If you work incessantly and have difficulty understanding, let alone prioritizing rest, then something in your thought life is amiss. Why else would we deprive ourselves of healthful and enjoyable parts of living?

If you keep making choices that take you further and further from what you truly want in life, and you never take a good look at what compels you, then how can you hope to choose differently?

In this section I talk about some mindsets that kept me working too hard for too long. That is, *fear,* and two of its rest-abolishing faces: *Performance and Perfectionism.*

Chapter Nine

Performance

Another huge hindrance to a lifestyle that prioritizes rest and sustainable life pace is the "performance" mindset as it pertains to our sense of self-worth. The standard of achievement that says you are important and vital if you can work hard enough, earn enough money, weigh a certain weight, close enough sales...the list goes on.[5]

This is not unlike the spending of our time, money and energy for possessions. It is the spending of our resources for an abstract idea, a label.

---

[5] Learn more about performing for self worth: https://www.psychologytoday.com/us/blog/what-mentally-strong-people-dont-do/201707/how-do-you-measure-your-self-worth

Sometimes we set the level of performance for ourselves and sometimes it is set for us by others.

Until we are ready to walk away from the driving need to be recognized and approved of, we will never fully embrace rest and change. You have to be willing to fail, to be disapproved of and judged. You need to hear the cry of your soul above the demands and pressures of what is expected of you and trust that voice.

The amazing thing about unlatching yourself from the restraints of performance expectations is that after a brief decline to recuperate and rest, the energy that waned is transformed, redirected and explodes with performance beyond past capacities!

In the Christian community there is a saying that we are sagely reminded of when life gets so busy that we find it impossible to stop and pray; "*You're too busy NOT to pray*". This is often followed up by a visual example of the person who is too busy to put gas in their car so they settle for pushing it everywhere they need to go. How silly! I would daresay that this applies to rest. If you are too busy and the drive to perform makes you think that you are impervious to the mortal, and the divinely-mandated, need for rest, then you are pushing your car in an effort to perform and neglecting the power of fuelling. Ironically, I dislike having to stop and perform the chore of fuelling my vehicle and often push it until my tank is dangerously low. Funny how that behaviour translates to other parts of life.

When we are soaring in our work, the last thing we want to do is voluntarily land and park the plane. "Keep flying!" We tell ourselves, "Use the momentum!" If we stop and take time to refuel, someone else may fly higher and better than we did. We will fall behind. This, of course, is a falsity. Flying until we drop out of the sky and crash will take us out of commission for much longer than a strategic stop for fuel ever would.

Consistency is key. That's another thing that I'm not very good at: consistency. Like many, I am a great starter. I fly high on the winds of inspiration going higher and higher only to find as the winds die away that my fuel tank is empty. Oh, if only I could master the art of consistency!

Before that, however, I need to know that my self worth does not come from what I do or how well I do it. I am valuable for who I am, who I belong to and who I am loved by. Nothing I can do will make me less valuable and nothing I can do will make me more valuable. I need to close my ears to any messages that tell me that I must look, act or be a certain way to be worthy. I need to find my value outside of my performance. What I am discovering is beautiful.

Chapter Ten

Perfectionism

While an unhealthy performance mindset tells us that we get our value from achievement; perfectionism drives us to a higher standard of completion.

The compulsion to get as much done as possible is compounded by the need for every activity to aspire to "perfect-ness". Perfection.

Perfectionism can actually inhibit performance completion because the perfectionist keeps rejecting the work in progress until it meets the elusive gold standard.[6]

---

[6] Read more about perfectionism:
https://www.psychologytoday.com/ca/basics/perfe
ctionism

Perhaps one of the most useful sayings I've adopted over the years is, "That's good enough, you won't see it from the expressway".

Perfectionism still surfaces. There are things that I will wrestle with to make as close to perfect as possible but I'm getting better at recognizing what is worth the effort and what is not.

There is a feeling I get when perfectionism is taking over. My jaw is set. My breathing is shallow. Everything becomes hyper focused on the task I'm trying to bring to final success. Just when I think it is good enough, I spot something off and I start fixing again. Frustration starts to build.

At some point I realize that its better to walk away. Take a look the next day. I've come to accept that anything I have to contribute in a tired, frustrated, hypertensive state is only going to compound my problem. Taking a break and coming back to the project rested with new perspective always brings a solution and joyful conclusion, if not an ability to accept a compromise.

My husband, Shawn, and I have worked side-by-side on home improvement projects for 26 years at the time of this writing. He is the pragmatic, economic, mathematician, technical expert and I am the aesthetics, general labourer, dreamer. A typical project starts with me saying, "Wouldn't it be great if..." or "This room would work better if... but it has to look nice."

Shawn, on the other hand, is looking at dollars and cents, how much time it will take, and if it will cause a domino effect of problems.

If he has his way the project will be done as economically as possible with less care to the aesthetics of the final result, whereas my way would look amazing but bankrupt us in the process.

We've had some doozy arguments over the years but I've come to realize that we are both right. If we both come with our individual perspective and discuss, negotiate, walk away, wait and repeat...we often find our way to a mutual sweet spot. We're literally better together. His idea would be a disaster. My idea would be a disaster. Our mutual idea is an amazing fusion of innovation and compromise.

I'll use our walk-in closet as an example.

We had a master bedroom that was large but awkward to use due to its shape. It really was like two bedrooms side-by-side and its long, narrow shape and entrance, windows and original closet placements made it almost impossible to use the full space as a bedroom.

We shifted the bed from one side to the other trying to find a comfortable room formation while grappling with the lack of closet and storage space. Finally, we decided that we would use half of the room for a standard bedroom and the other side would become a generous walk-in closet.

It took years before the progression of renovations and finances would allow for us to build our walk-in closet then it took us almost a year to come to an agreement on how the closet would be built.

We saved 50% immediately by moving away from a well-known closet shelving brand and going with a different manufacturer. At first, I balked because I thought the quality of the shelving would be inferior but I used a phrase over and over that really helped, "It's just a closet". I mean, I wanted it to be beautiful, organized, impressive AND sturdy but I realized with Shawn's help that the quality of the manufacturers wasn't that different.

We gathered around the computer screen as we entered the dimensions of our closet space and began designing the layout with the manufacturer's design program. That was when it got really tough. I wanted deep drawers, not shallow, small ones, so I asked for the deep closet shelves. Shawn balked because lining the room with deep closet shelving ate up the centre space.

Initially, I wanted a place to sit in the centre but when we tallied up what we needed for hanging clothes and storing shoes...there wasn't enough for drawers. There was also some unusable space under a window.

There were problems and disagreements. We would talk and Shawn would redesign. We would look and get frustrated and walk away.

We did this over and over until we came to a mutual agreement on the design. In the end we both got what we wanted. It involved some creative thinking (me) and some customization

(Shawn). In the end, we got a fabulous walk-in closet that suits us both and maximized the space efficiently.

Neither of us could've achieved that alone. It happened over time with lots of rest and perspective.

The closet isn't perfect though. There are a few things that I still have to close my eyes to and pretend aren't there. Most people wouldn't notice but, of course, I do. Shawn does as well.

The point is, it's a closet. We do show our closet to friends because we're so thrilled with it but at the end of the day, it's a place to store clothes and shoes that we can close the door on.

If you struggle with perfectionism, it's important to separate yourself from it. It's okay to strive for excellence in what you do but if that striving is not sustainable, you are at risk. Something is going to suffer. Life isn't perfect. We can't bring our A-game to every sphere of life.

It's about choices and seasons.

Chapter Eleven

Fear

I t is alarming to realize that, for many of us, the basis of many decisions is fear[7]. Even though most of our decisions are rooted in pain or pleasure, it is actually the "fear" of pain and the "promise" of pleasure that activate a lot of our choices.

I had a conversation with a friend where they were being put in a situation that conflicted with their faith. At first, they focused on their desire to love as their reason for staying in that situation. As we talked, however, it slipped out that they were afraid of rejection if they left that situation because of their faith.

---

[7] Read more about fear:
https://www.psychologytoday.com/ca/blog/the-main-ingredient/200909/the-most-powerful-motivator

I reminded them that fear is a terrible dictator when it comes to matters of faith and the compromising of it, but I understand their dilemma having lived through the consequences of trying to navigate a similar situation. The pain is all too real and lasting. I wouldn't wish it on anyone. I promised to pray for them to make the right choice for the right reasons.

It's important to know that you can be doing the right thing for the wrong reasons. You can be staying in a marriage because you are afraid to leave, not because you are committed to making the relationship work.

You can be staying in a job because you are afraid to leave and face failure. You stay in body but your heart is long gone and your work begins to show that fact.

You can stay in your church or community outlet because exiting opens you up to judgement instead of launching out to do what God has put in your heart. So, you stay and live in silent opposition to your situation.

Fear hides behind many virtuous faces but it is still fear, and fear is the opposite of faith. Fear needs to be addressed.

Hard conversations need to be had. Risks need to be taken and choices need to be made.

You aren't doing anyone, including yourself, any favours by walking the fence. I'm not saying that leaving is always the answer but staying with a growing unresolved conflict in your heart is not "doing the right thing" either.

A lot of us can pinpoint a situation in our lives where we are caught in a double-bind; a situation where we feel trapped between two impossible results; a lose, lose.

I learned this concept from a program called "The Genesis Process[8]" and it changed my life.

You see, I was caught between a wonderful job and my feelings of wanting to leave it; that was my double-bind. On one hand I was feeling lonely and confined, like I had hit a performance and reward ceiling, and felt uninspired by the industry work I was doing. On the other hand, it paid our bills, was flexible in hours, fulfilling an important mission, and was an ideal

---

[8] Learn more about the Genesis Process: https://www.genesisprocess.org/

position for someone like me without formal post secondary education. I should have felt blessed to have such a great career and be treated as well as I was. Yet, I felt trapped and unhappy. It didn't help that my husband would say I could leave, but we would likely be forced to sell our current home for a lesser one if I did. I didn't want to make a decision that could result in us giving up our family home.

For years I shoved down my growing discontent and desire to leave to stay and do "the right thing". I was an adult, not a child, and this was the grown-up thing to do. Still, my unhappiness was growing and my despair was finding outlets. I cried a lot. As soon as I entered my empty office every day and looked around, I would burst into tears.

I spoke to a trusted friend who was adept at the Genesis program and I shared my double-bind with her. She listened to my "lose, lose" situation quietly and when I was done, she said that I was leaving out one factor: God. It felt a little idealistic and honestly, her words hit me like a punch in the gut. My work was considered "God-business" so the idea that God could work out an outcome that would allow me to leave my job without me losing our home was something I hadn't considered before. I was genuinely shocked at that thought.

I didn't take action immediately but her faith-inspiring words remained with me. God cares about me and if I don't fit neatly in this way of serving Him through my job, He might be gracious enough to allow me to rest and find a way to serve Him alternatively without having the financial consequences one might expect. This sounded impossible and in order to take the risk, I would need to summon faith.

Unfortunately, I shelved that and continued to find ways to cope with my present situation. I tried my best. It wasn't until pain built up in unbearable levels in other areas of my life before I finally decided that taking the risk to leave was better than the pain of staying. I had reached a place where the potential consequences of leaving didn't matter as much to me anymore. I was prepared to lose everything.

Instinctively, I knew this was the beginning of a new future and as soon as I wrote my resignation letter, the name of this book came to mind and I reserved the LeavingBusy.com domain name and social media accounts. Even if my life spiralled out of control and self-destructed because of my choice, I was going to document it and share it with the world.

The funniest thing happened though. After an initial "what did I just do?" panic and enduring skeptical looks and raised eyebrows at my unconventional decision, I experienced a flicker of something I hadn't felt in a very long time: *Hope*.

Chapter Twelve

On the Basis of Sex

Even as I boldly embarked on a journey back to a traditional role and dependence on my husband, I began contemplating the changes in society that made my decision seem so radical.

Incidentally, I happened upon a movie called "On the Basis of Sex". It is *inspired by* the true story of Ruth Bader Ginsburg who is currently an American lawyer and jurist who is an Associate Justice of the U.S. Supreme Court.

The movie follows her journey as a struggling attorney and new mother who faces adversity and numerous obstacles in her fight for equal rights. When Ruth takes on a ground-breaking tax case with her husband, attorney Martin Ginsburg, she knows it could change the direction of her career and the way the courts view gender discrimination.[9]

The story was very entertaining and enlightening but it portrayed a pivotal scene in which opponents to her argument for gender equality brainstormed all the negative effects that this change would have on society. I was incredulous because every single one of these arguments presented in the screenplay actually happened! I remember looking at my husband and pausing the movie to discuss this scene and speculate how it failed to arouse the sense of falsity that it was likely designed to.

This is an excerpt taken from the screenplay written by Daniel Stiepleman featuring the thematic scene where Erwin Griswald (Solicitor General and Dean of Harvard University) along with Ernest J. Brown and James Bozarth (Department of Justice Tax Division Appellate Section) are discussing the adverse effects of gender equality as negatively affecting the American family:

---

[9]

http://www.imperialvalleymall.com/article/12541

BROWN (to Bozarth) *Paint the judges a picture of the America that will exist if they rule the wrong way. Children running home from school to find... No one's there. Mommy's at the office. Or on a factory floor.*

GRISWOLD *That's very good, Ernie. If a man and woman vie for the same job, she can work for less. What is a man without a paycheck to take care of his family?*

BROWN *What woman would want him?*

BOZARTH (going with their flow) *Wages go down. Divorce rates soar. Society unravels.*

BROWN *Exactly! The other side wants this to be about the Equal Protection Principle. YOU need to show the court that what's really at stake is the American family.*

GRISWOLD *What the judges are deciding is what kind of country, what kind of society, they want their children and grandchildren to grow up in.*

As I stated, these arguments presented as part of the movie script opposing legal gender equality proved to be TRUE!

Divorce rates show a dramatic increase in the 1970's around the time that women's legal gender equality began.[10]

The health of our children has declined. This could be attributed to children coming home everyday to an empty home and engaging in "safe" indoor activities like watching television and playing video games until parents arrive home later after work. According to research, the number of obese and overweight children between six and twelve years of age has DOUBLED in the past 30 years![11]

Now, I am not against gender equality. I am grateful to be alive during a period of history where women can vote, be educated, work in all fields, and have the same legal protection as men.

10

https://familyinequality.wordpress.com/2018/09/15/the-coming-divorce-decline/

11

https://www.slideshare.net/mobile/coachdaisha/5-dangerous-realities-adults-face-with-obese-latchkey-children-in-america

Having said that, an honest look at our marriages, home life and children's health reveals that we have paid a terrible price for the void left in the quest for freedom and equality.

I personally do not care who stays home and who goes to work every day to earn the family income. However, I firmly believe that someone needs to take on the supportive, nurturing role at home without shame or discrimination for the sake of our family life.

Why should our children be left at daycares to be raised by strangers as early as one year old so both parents can work? Why should children eat breakfasts furnished by breakfast programs at school instead of at home?[12] Why should children come home to an empty home after school to fend for themselves while their parents finish their workday? Why should mealtimes consist of frozen convenience food eaten alone, in front of the television? Why should marriages break up due to the crushing pressures of two competing careers, raising a family and trying to manage a home while two people who love each other drift

---

[12] https://slideplayer.com/slide/8796585/

apart?[13] What kind of country and society have we created for our children and grandchildren?

I understand that sometimes two parents have to work to survive but survival isn't typically what we sacrifice our family life for.

We sacrifice the well-being of our families for expensive phones, vacations, dining out, and a plethora of material and social non-necessities. We want bigger and better.

Dual income families have become the norm: the standard that single-income families can never attain and are viewed inferior to.

Am I suggesting that we roll back equality and force women back into the home? No. I'm simply pointing out that every family should evaluate its priorities and determine if one parent or the other should voluntarily relinquish their rights for the betterment of the family. This is a choice that can only be determined by each couple for themselves and their children.

13

https://www.wsj.com/articles/SB1000142405270230
3544604576430341393583056

It may not be right for every family, for every home, but I know in my heart that it is right for us. I learned this after 10 years of trying to live up to the modern expectation of the woman working outside the home as an equal provider. I wish I could go back and choose differently. It wasn't worth it.

So now, even though it is later in life, I feel privileged to stay home and be the primary caregiver to my family while my husband works to provide for us. I am grateful that I wasn't forced, that laws provide for me to choose to work if I so wish. I just know that life is better for my husband, myself and my children when I am free to be home instead.

Contemplation of Part 999

1. Do you feel caught in a lose-lose situation? If so, explain.

2. In what ways is fear holding you back from living the life that you long for?

3. Have you ever felt the relief of making a hard decision? If so, explain.

4. Do you ever find yourself getting caught up in trying to please people? If so, how does this play out in your life?

5. Do you have a good grasp of your value outside what you do?

6. Have you ever been caught up in perfectionism in any area of your life? If so, explain.

7. Can you share an example of where you produced something less than perfect in an effort to focus on your priorities?

8. In our modern dual income society, what do you think about one person opting to stay home?

9. Do you think your family could learn to live on one income in order to make one person staying home feasible?

10. Is there anyone in your household that would be willing to make the sacrifice of a career to take care of other household members and make a comfortable home?

11. Do you think the designated care-giver could manage their time wisely and be treated with respect in all decisions regardless of their earning deficit?

Notes

_____

_____

_____

_____

_____

_____

_____

_____

_____

_____

_____

Part IV: Setting the Record Straight

Chapter Thirteen

Lazy or Wise

There are some readers who will read this book and use it as a license to shirk responsibility to their family or to let go of obligations that they didn't want anyway. They weren't really working wholeheartedly in the first place and this call to rest only feeds the desire to be lazy.

There is another segment of readers who will read my words and it will answer the thirsty cry of their heart for a long-desired reprieve. They will want to put some of my recommendations into action but the false mindsets discussed in the last section will disallow them to put down their burdens for even a moment. If they do try to rest, they will obsess constantly about whether they made the right decision or if they are the lazy person I just described.

The last category of readers will dismiss my book as idealistic, unattainable or plain error leading to sloth and selfish living. They will look at all they do and achieve and they feel that stepping back for any significant rest is impossible. They are certain it will have an irreversible detrimental effect on themselves, others and their goals. Building rhythms of work and rest and adhering to the rest part as firmly as the work part seems sinful, wrong or irresponsible.

I live in the midst of these opinions. There are days where I question my choice to rest and to continue living life at a slower pace even to the point of encouraging others to do the same in this writing. I came up with this series of questions to help me remember my original reasoning and separate from the expectations and mindsets that drove me to overwork in the past.

1. Do I have a history of being a hard worker or being lazy?

Have you ever had a friend going through a difficult time ask you if they are crazy? The tongue in cheek answer is that if you're concerned that you might be crazy, then it is a sign that you are not because crazy people don't have such self doubts! I think the same can be true with laziness. Truly lazy people don't see themselves as lazy. They can refuse to work, wasting all their time on fruitless activities and they are oblivious to their sloth.

Meanwhile there is a person who works compulsively and is producing at every level and constantly sits in anxiety when saying no to the expectations of others for so much as an hour. The call to work is so strong that they literally cannot enjoy their rest.

That's why instead of going by your feelings, why not look at your pay stubs or your achievements on a daily, weekly, monthly, seasonal, or annual basis as evidence that you might be eligible for some well-deserved rest.

2. Did I set my hand to work for a reasonable period before claiming this rest?

How much rest you take or don't take and what it looks like is completely up to you and your unique situation but here are examples of some reasonable rest periods in relation to work:

- Daily: 12.5 hours of work, errands, chores etc. / 2.5-4.5 hours of leisure (including some physical activity) / 7-9 hours of sleep.[14]

- Weekly: Six days of work, errands, chores, volunteer work etc. before a day off to enjoy worship, family, friends and solitude. (following the Bible's Sabbath model)

- Annually: When was your vacation? If its been more than a year, you're overdue.[15]

- Life Stages: Six or more years of work coupled with significant increase in life stress could indicate the benefit of taking a year off. (following the Bible's Sabbatical model)

The more significant lengths of rest can also be quantified and mandated by your ability to conserve during your working

---

[14] Read research paper on preferred amount of daily leisure time:
https://papers.ssrn.com/sol3/papers.cfm?abstract_id=3285436
[15] Read more about importance of taking vacations:
https://www.cnn.com/travel/article/why-vacations-matter/index.html

periods so that you can afford the rest time. Setting aside some of your income for a vacation or sabbatical is necessary. A sabbatical may not be feasible for everyone but the other rest times are fairly standard for most people.

3. How am I spending my rest time?

How you spend your rest time is extremely important. This is your precious opportunity to do the things that work and obligations deprive you of doing. These are your sacred moments to drink deeply of life's beauty and tap into the creativity and renewal of purpose that true rest provides.

I'm not against commercial pleasures such as amusement parks, shopping malls, television, video games and the like. I have partaken in them myself with great enjoyment. However, when I dreamed of taking a year off it wasn't so I could binge-watch all of Netflix or smash every level of Candy Crush! I wanted to organize my home, get healthy and write a book!

What I'm saying is that my year of rest wasn't rest from *all* labours exactly. It was a rest from a certain type of work and the picking up of different activities that I felt called to do. For some it might be the opportunity to plant and tend a garden, take classes to explore their love of painting, or complete a hike of epic proportions.

What you choose to do during any season of rest says a lot about you and your life goals but none so much as when you take a whole year of your life to invest in whatever you desire most.

4. What is the purpose of taking this time and am I accomplishing it?

It is highly likely that what you intend to do on your time off may give way to something completely unexpected. I had initially thought of doing a "day in my life" type vlog to track my sabbatical but then quickly decided against it. The chore of daily taping, editing, posting and answering comments would quickly eat up the actual time I should be living.

I did want to write a book during my year off but soon learned that starting a blog was going to be part of that process. I didn't plan to start a blog but I found that it was the most amazing adventure. The website creation and launching consumed three full months of time investment before I felt comfortable pressing the pause button to pay attention to this writing project.

Many times, during that three-month period, as I worked as hard on my blog as anything I had ever accomplished in the workplace, I wondered if I had gotten lost in my rest goals. I saw the potential to derail my rest objectives and other goals I had and made the necessary adjustments to make sure I didn't lose my way.

It's important to assess and reassess constantly to make sure you don't end your specified measure of rest tired and regretful of how you used your precious time. So far, I have zero regrets. Everything I'm investing in my blog and this book have fulfilled life desires I've held dear. Even if the world does not receive my work as being a success, and it never becomes notable in any way, my year of pursuing a life goal will be immeasurably successful to me.

5. What has the result been from taking this rest? Good or bad?

I have no idea what will follow this year sabbatical but even if I cannot maintain a living through my writing fully on my terms and find myself once again working full-time out of necessity, it will have been worth it. You can bet I will do everything I can to budget and save for another sabbatical seven to ten years from now to do it all again.

If full-time employment becomes necessary, I will hold the memories of this special time in my heart when the phone is ringing, deadlines are looming and I'm back to frantically dashing into the grocery store to get dinner fixings before going home.

Of course, I have high hopes of continuing as I am now, writing for a few hours at home with time to exercise, clean, cook and see friends without the hustle and bustle.

Whatever the outcome, nothing of this year will be lost. I have changed. My life outlook has changed. My life goals have changed. The Melissa who emerges from this year of rest is vastly different from the woman who entered it, in a good way. I have grown in confidence and perspective.

This is a great assessment tool. Is your life better? Are you making better choices? Have you experienced positive change? What about your loved ones? Would you trade this experience for a material thing?

As for those who would wield spiritual superiority and say that rest is lazy or selfish, I would encourage you to look at the many Bible scriptures that advocate rest with new eyes. Rest is very biblical, spiritual and Godly. This is covered more in the "Spiritual Perspective" section of this book.

"Come unto me, all ye that labour and are heavy laden,

and I will give you rest.

Take my yoke upon you, and learn of me; for I am meek and

lowly in heart: and ye shall find rest unto your souls.

For my yoke is easy, and my burden is light."

Matthew 11:28-30 KJV

Chapter Fourteen

Us Four and No More

When aspiring to the rest and peace that a slowed down lifestyle has to offer, there is a lot of refusal to engage with people and activities around you that would sabotage that way of life. On the other hand, there is some moral and social obligation to reach outside ourselves and offer something of value to the world around us. Weighing my need for refreshment and my social limits, I've had to come to terms with what I have to offer and when it is time to put up the no vacancy sign. This is a dance that anyone serious about sustainable paced living will need to do.

We live in a unique time in history where our world is expanded in a way it has never been before. Going back to the early pioneer days, a family's children had one set of parents, one teacher at a time and no Internet. By comparison, today we are juggling multiple sets of parents, often multiple schools with each student having a variety of teachers and the world at our fingertips.

Every contact from family, school, work, place of worship, market, hobby, friendship etc. has a voice, an agenda. All of them are calling to us for connection, for purchase, for help and for awareness. It can be dizzying and lead to a sense of never being enough.

How do we sort through the necessary demands and desired connections to leave room for the health of our inner life? The temptation can be to put up barbed wire fence, go off social media, and abandon our phones to go off the grid. I'm laughing because some of you just got excited at the idea of doing that! But no, we don't want to become hermits — selfish people concerned only about ourselves while others suffer for lack of our engagement with the world.

I have a few opinions on this based on my own experience and I share them not so you can follow them as an absolute guide but so that you can contemplate what works for you in your unique life.

Have you heard the term, "not my circus, not my monkeys"? When I feel demands coming my way that other people have created and they are completely capable of taking care of themselves or finding another able-bodied person to take care of, then I say no. It's important to distinguish the nuances of this though. I have some excellent examples from my real life to share.

A few days ago, I asked a friend to go for coffee and during that visit I shared with her that I no longer wanted to admin a Facebook group I had created because the theme no longer was relevant to me. I considered her because she was still very passionate about that theme and I thought she might be interested in taking over the group rather than me just shutting it down.

My friend wisely took a breath and delayed her decision for a few months. We agreed that there would be no harm in just shutting the group down if she decided not to take the lead at that time.

I created this group, not my friend. She accepted my invitation to join it but she never accepted to take responsibility for it. My decision that this group was now irrelevant to me and her remaining interest in the group focus in no way obligates her to take on my duties as an administrator. Not her circus, not her monkeys. Right?

Her refusal to blindly say yes to my request didn't make things awkward or jeopardize our relationship. In fact, I have respect for her decision and know that if she does say yes in a couple months, it will be a well contemplated decision. I also know that if she says no, then life will go on even if I have to archive that group.

Another friend was having brake trouble on their vehicle in the bitter winter months. Lacking the money to go to a mechanic, her husband was going to do the brake job himself. They needed a garage to do the work in. It was a very inconvenient time for us due to renovations and water heater issues but I recognized the urgency of the situation. We put the garage heaters on and accepted their call for a warm place to do the repairs.

See the difference between these two examples? Both were technically "not our circus and not our monkeys", but one was important to intervene and the other was not.

Here's another set of examples.

We had friends years ago who were not good with their money. Through our friendship we learned that they had borrowed a significant amount of money from an aged relative and not paid it back. They were not paying their bills and were near bankruptcy. They then decided to take a vacation trip and we babysat one of their children while they went away. Upon return they asked us for a loan of money.

We wanted their friendship and we wanted to help them but we knew the likelihood of the money being repaid was low and that we would resent them for not repaying it as we had our own financial difficulties at the time. We were also making spending sacrifices that they were unwilling to make for themselves. We said no and I did feel a bit of chill in the relationship after that but it was the right decision. Unfortunately, their life situation did unravel, and we lost the friendship as it was, but I know it wasn't our fault. We had given all we had to give at that time of our life and they had made their own decisions.

On the other hand, there is a person we know who has made poor decisions throughout their life and can be very difficult to be around due to their hygiene and behaviours. We have established some boundaries but try to help them as much as possible because we sense that some of their issues stem from mental illness or cognitive delay. They are disadvantaged to some degree and are so far down the path of their choices that merciful help is better suited than tough love.

How do we sift through the chaos and determine where we should invest our precious time and resources and where we should conserve it? I guarantee you will make better decisions if you have some excess time and resources to give. The truth is there are no hard and fast rules as to where you should extend mercy and when you should love by allowing a person to face their challenges without your intervention. What I do know is that both approaches are important. We do not serve others or ourselves by playing the martyr and rescuing others from their choices without discrimination.

I used to find myself scrutinizing people in need and looking only for those who had not contributed to their own demise as suitable candidates for my help. What I learned was that there are very few people in that category. Innocent victims of misfortune are out there but most people have had a hand in the circumstances that bring them to their place of need.

Now, my decision to help or not help is based more on the persons treatment of others and how they attempt to contribute to the world around them. Even if they make poor choices, if their heart is one of wanting to do better and trying to help others, I can be more charitable.

We have all been recipients of mercy even if we think we have accomplished our success on our own. We may think we have made all the tough choices to arrive where we are and others need to shape up and do the same, but none of us do it alone.

At the very least, there is a perfect God who has looked at mankind in its sin and self destruction and still deemed us as worthy of mercy. He sent His perfect and holy Son to be born, live and die a horrific death even though He did nothing to deserve it. He had spent His brief, earthly life inspiring, serving and healing people. His crime was telling the truth of who He was and He was turned over to Roman crucifixion by His own people.

Whether you believe or don't believe, whatever life we have achieved even now, over 2000 years later, was affected by that event. That is why we are bound to extend mercy to others outside ourselves and our immediate family, even as we shoulder the responsibilities of our own circus and monkeys.

Chapter Fifteen

The Busy Sloth

I had an experience that is very personal to me but I am sharing it because it revealed a very important truth.

At the beginning of my initial prayer and fasting journey I took some time every day to repent for behaviours and flaws I was aware of. After a few days of this I woke up and before I opened my eyes, I asked the Holy Spirit to reveal what issue I should repent of on this particular day. Instantly, in my mind I saw what looked like a black screen with the words SLOTH in huge, bold, red lettering. I was a bit taken aback and I did a mind shift like the flipping of a slide to another more known character flaw. After all, I AM NOT A LAZY PERSON! Then I stopped. I should at least examine this initial picture a bit more closely. Why would that impression have come to my mind when it is so at odds with how I see myself?

I did a little Google search of "sin of sloth" and I didn't connect with many of the results but I did come across an article that caught my attention. This article described sloth in terms that were very applicable to me. It described sloth not so much by inactivity but in choosing activities more on personal preference than on God's priorities.[16]

I saw the many mornings where I jump into action attacking my long to-do list but neglecting to sit for even 15 minutes to pray and read my Bible; the days I packed with errands but was incapable of connecting with people on a meaningful level; the Sundays where I dragged myself half-heartedly to church to "get it over with" so I was free to get on with my own pursuits.

Certainly, God was looking past the flurry of activity and seeing straight into the motivations of my heart. It felt

---

[16] Read more about sloth:
https://www.christianheadlines.com/columnists/james-tonkowich/you-re-probably-more-slothful-than-you-realize.html

uncomfortable and disconcerting to see myself in this perspective.

I went downstairs brooding over this and my husband asked what was going on in my head. I mentioned that I felt convicted of being a sloth and he reacted dramatically, "You are not a SLOTH!".

I simply gave him the article I had just read and he changed his tune just as I had.

That revelation motivated me to get extremely involved in our church's prayer ministry and volunteering for weekend encounters. I didn't want to be a sloth so I filled up my non-work time with more spiritually-oriented activities and put aside all personal pursuits. My intentions were good but, true to my nature, it was an all or nothing approach.

A couple years and some perspective later, I realize that we all tend to gravitate toward activity and work that we enjoy while avoiding activity and work that we don't. I interpreted this gentle correction in a way that was dramatic and unsustainable to the point that when I embarked on my sabbatical, I couldn't pray or read my Bible at all. I was so burnt out on this pathway to God that all I could do was play beginner chords on the keyboard and sing worship songs for a while. It was raw, pure and holy.

I'll be honest that it is only now that I feel the desire to return to regular prayer and Bible reading as part of my daily rhythm. This may sound like a terrible admission for someone who claims to have faith but I think it is more prevalent among modern-day believers than most people want to admit.

Many of us take our days like empty jars and fill them with the large rocks, stones, pebbles, sand and water that represent priorities of our choosing[17]. Some of us are better at prioritizing than others and thus are able to fill our days with more or at least get the most important things done. Others fill their days with just the smaller, more urgent or pleasurable stuff and never fit the other elements in.

I think this is where the rhythm of work and rest coupled with the priorities of faith brings balance to our choices. It is

---

[17] Read entire time management analogy: https://www.developgoodhabits.com/rock-pebbles-sand/

possible to work and rest exactly as prescribed in the Bible and completely miss the heart of the One who designed us and the world we live in. I also think it is possible to sincerely love and attempt to serve God and completely miss His call to balance work and rest in a sustainable way.

Like many of the paradoxes mentioned in this book, we need to prayerfully study, pray and reflect to ensure we are being judicious and faithful stewards of our time here on Earth and the bodies we've been blessed with.

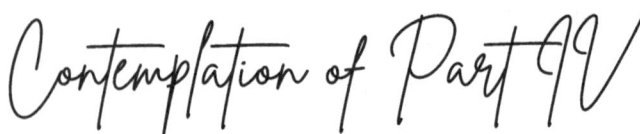

Contemplation of Part IV

1. Do you agree that taking measured rest and living a more manageable lifestyle is being lazy or wise? Why?

2. Do you agree with the examples of measured rest versus periods of work? If not, which ones and why?

3. If you do agree with the examples of measured rest versus periods of work, do you practise them? Why or why not?

4. Do you ever struggle with feeling guilty when you take time to rest?

5. Do you ever feel like your efforts to enjoy rest are sabotaged? If so by whom and how?

6. When you have periods of discretionary rest time, how do you opt to spend it?

7. If you were given the opportunity to have an entire year to rest from work and minimize your duties in all areas of life, how would you spend it?

8. If you took that year to rest, what do you think the consequences and/or benefits would be?

9. Do you have established boundaries when it comes to when and how you will help others? If so, what are they?

10. Have you ever taken on responsibility for something that was really someone else's responsibility? If so, how did that make you feel?

11. Have you ever helped someone in spite of the fact that they contributed to their own problem? If so, how did that make you feel?

12. If you were enjoying a period of rest and someone asked you to take on a project, would you be able to say no? If no, explain.

13. Have you ever found yourself too busy to pray or read your Bible? If yes, what are the activities and why did they feel more important?

14. Do you tend to serve God busily and yet feel that somehow you missed the true purpose of your faith? If so, please explain.

15. Do you feel that you make good use of your time in general? If no, please explain.

16. Do you feel that your priorities line up fully with your faith? If no, please explain.

17. How do you feel if you set down your priorities to take on things that are important to God? Please explain.

Notes

Part V: The Lost Art of Rest

Chapter Sixteen

Turn, Turn, Turn

"To every thing there is a season,

and a time to every purpose under the heaven:

A time to be born, and a time to die; a time to plant,

and a time to pluck up that which is planted;

A time to kill, and a time to heal;

a time to break down, and a time to build up;

A time to weep, and a time to laugh;

a time to mourn, and a time to dance;

A time to cast away stones,

and a time to gather stones together;

a time to embrace, and a time to refrain from embracing;

A time to get, and a time to lose;

a time to keep, and a time to cast away;

A time to rend, and a time to sew;

a time to keep silence, and a time to speak;

A time to love, and a time to hate;

a time of war, and a time of peace."

Ecclesiastes 3:1-8 (KJV)

There is a song by the Byrds that literally quotes this ancient Bible passage word for word. It's called Turn! Turn! Turn! In fact, those are the only words NOT in the original Bible passage!

I've come to recognize and pay attention to life seasons in a way I failed to in my youth. When I was young, I forged ahead with plans with little regard for the appropriate timing of my ventures. Inevitably I would find myself trying to accomplish something in the wrong season!

- I'd want to paint the outside of the house when it was too hot or too cold.

- I'd plan to rake the leaves but the snow would cover them before I had a chance.

- We'd start renovations inside when the weather was ideal for projects outside.

- I'd wash our vehicle just before a rainstorm.

- Shawn would be forced to complete the winter tune up of our vehicles outdoors after the weather had gotten too frigid for this.

It took years to learn through trials, mistakes and interrupted plans that seasons matter. It is strategic to look ahead to the seasons and our goals to determine when is the best time to plan the work.

- The seasons of weather show us the changing of life.

- Spring is full of new life in plants and in animals. It is a time to sow.

- Summer is hot with cooler times in the morning and evening.

- Autumn is about harvesting and preparing for winter.

- Winter is cold and barren.

You can't plant your garden in the winter. You don't ski in the summer. You don't harvest berries and apples in the spring. You don't typically put out lawn furniture in the fall.

Even now, I've become more watchful of the weather to seize the beautiful days perfect for outside work or enjoyment so that I can focus on indoor projects on the less suitable ones. I've come to realize why many structured activities disband over the summer...even hobbies like knitting prefer the winter months while gardening prefers the summer.

Seasons are not just about weather. Life is a series of seasons. Childhood, adolescence, young adulthood, young married, young parenthood, teen parenthood, empty nest and retirement. All life seasons have different flows and goals. We can accomplish things out of season but life typically works better when we cooperate with the seasons instead of fight them.

We know these things, so why do we try to live our lives as though we only have one season?

Is there never a time to start certain activities and end others?

Do we make time for the different seasons of life?

It's okay to let go of activities that lend themselves to one season and move on to other ones. I used to think that if you were committed, you had to forge unhindered through every season. No relenting. No stopping. No changing. No switching.

Now I realize how completely frustrating and false that notion was. We're not meant to do everything in every season!

An example of this was the garden I planted in my backyard every spring. The children were young and liked playing outside with their friends. I would toil in my backyard garden and with every year, I tried to expand it. I took photos and posted them on Facebook with joy and pride. Nothing tasted as good as those fruits and veggies and I would share my surplus with my neighbours. As my children grew, I recruited their help in watering and harvesting.

The weeds were my nemesis. I would patiently pluck every little weed by hand to get at the roots and fill buckets with them. My body would ache from the hours bent over or kneeling in the sun and my hands and arms reacted to all the natural compounds they were being exposed to.

We live in a highly naturalized area so squirrels, rabbits and birds helped themselves to my strawberries even if I hung them. We built a fence around the garden to keep them out. Later the fence kept my dog from digging in the soil and eating my tomatoes.

Just when I thought I had everything protected, the Japanese beetles arrived. This was a new challenge. I went out every day to catch and drown them but their destruction of my raspberry bush, corn, cherry tree and basil was relentless. I noticed my pear tree had orange-rust marks on the leaves and after some research realized that this phenomenon happens when a pear tree is planted near certain coniferous trees that are abundant in our neighbourhood. After almost 10 years I have yet to enjoy a pear from that tree even though it produces an abundance for the worms and birds to enjoy.

As I was waging this annual battle my children grew up and playing outside was no longer part of their leisure time. I found myself alone in my garden except for the times I begged my husband and son to help me with the weeding.

I wondered about all the time and energy I was investing in growing a garden when I could easily pick up the produce at the local market or join an organized grow co-op. I was working full time and it no longer made sense to spend my valuable time off the way I had in the past.

I looked out at my yard void of young children playing and realized that I had lost my grace for gardening. All the joy and wonder had gone out of it. No-one else in the household cared and I was tired of doing it all alone.

We decided to invest in some landscaping and that spring my garden disappeared for good, covered with grass, bushes and stone. We re-purposed the bricks that had surrounded it. It was a bittersweet sign that the seasons had changed in my life. As much as I had relished tending a garden in the past, I no longer had the heart to continue.

This sounds incredibly sad and it was. It was only one of the first changes that were made in response to a shift in our family life. I still have tender feelings about my children growing up and moving on but trying to hold on to vestiges of that season wasn't working. I needed to let go.

I have great memories of those days and miss parts of them a lot but I don't regret my decision to stop gardening. Even this year of sabbatical didn't tempt me to start up again. By letting go of the work of gardening, it has freed up time for other activities like the writing that I am doing now. In fact, I read recently about a writer who just sold her dream farm because it kept her too busy to write.

Making more time to write wasn't my objective when I let the garden dream take its last rattling breath. I just knew it was the end and I didn't know what was coming next. It didn't fit my life anymore. At the time it felt as though my entire life was ending. I couldn't see the future and that unsettled me greatly.

Now though, it makes perfect sense that something incredibly special to me needed to die so a new specialness could emerge. My daily joy just changed forms. I'm still sowing, weeding and harvesting...it's just ideas and words now instead of seeds and plants.

Will I ever garden again? If I do it won't be like before. It will be a few pots or a single raised bed. There are no plans or desire at this point.

If you are experiencing a sunset on a season of your life, feel the grief as you say your goodbyes but take heart, my friend, a new season will be rising and your tears will become joy in the morning!

Chapter Seventeen

Daily Rest

Even though this book is not focused on sleep and physical rest, it's imperative to discuss the importance of daily rest and how to maximize it. For years I embraced the mindset that sleep was somehow a waste of time and that the truly disciplined, productive person would strive to survive on as little as possible. I designed schedules that set my rising time at 4:30am so I could have exercise AND a quiet time of prayer and Bible study before the day officially began. I was convinced that the secret to spirituality, fitness and the person I wanted to be was on the other side of disciplining myself to maintain this perfect schedule. I was endlessly frustrated with myself when I inevitably failed after a week or two.

I would be sleepy, grumpy, miserable and ineffective. I developed a dependence on caffeinated beverages. I was angry and frustrated with myself and others. When I think of how I was tormenting myself and causing hormonal chaos by trying to live up to a perfect life standard that wasn't sustainable, it makes me incredibly sad. If I could go back in time, I would assure my younger self that it was okay to live a life that allowed for eight full hours of sleep. Life success isn't dependant on a perfectly fit and groomed body, clean house, hours of spiritual activity and all else that I was trying so desperately to be and never could manage.

As I have aged, I've come to embrace my sleep as vital to my health and I part-take without guilt, knowing it is a foundation to my emotional and physical wellbeing. I still want to incorporate all the other elements of life but I now know that cutting sleep is not an option.

To our credit, my husband and I did a lot of things right in the sleep department.

We agreed to never allow a television or food into the bedroom. The bedroom was a place for sleep and intimacy only.

This dedicated usage of our sleep space serves an important purpose of signalling our brain and body as to our purpose when we enter it each evening. In fact, I have to be careful not to hang out in my bedroom too much during the day because the very sight of my bed begins a lulling, beckoning to sleep that is very powerful. Other than to put clothing away, dust or pass through to my private bathroom, I don't hang out in that room if I plan to be productive.

I don't nap very often even though I am currently home and able to. The reason for this is that when I lay down for a nap, I fall into a 2-3-hour deep sleep that disrupts my ability to fall into and remain asleep at my regular time. It's better for me to go to bed an hour earlier or rise an hour later than to have a nap. When I am ill, or extremely sleep deprived, I do nap but for me, there is always a consequence to my night-time sleep if I take.

My husband is different. He can do those 20-30-minute cat naps and function fine afterwards. He seems genuinely refreshed and it doesn't affect his night sleep. Since he has less flexibility about sleeping in, those naps are vital to his well-being. In my sleep deprived years, I was endlessly frustrated by his ability to shut down for naps and his lack of willingness to short-cut sleep to get things done. Life has taught me the wisdom of his choices and to respect the differences between our sleep habits.

We use light-blocking blinds and have full darkness to increase our melatonin production. Anything that would have a power light, we purchased stickers that filter and dim that light significantly.

We mute our phones to avoid being woken by random text alerts during our sleep. In case our children need us, we have given them a private home line number and it is not muted. If that phone rings, we know we are dealing with a personal emergency and are happy to be disrupted.

Some things we could work on is the recommendation to put aside screen time in the couple hours preceding bedtime. We've tried but we do still like to watch television, surf social media, etc...; up to bedtime. Occasionally we do other activities like listen to music and I've done adult colouring books and knitting but even our reading is on a screen so we haven't been perfectly successful. Like most people, these last hours of the day are the precious remnants of a busy schedule and we value using them for activities that we personally enjoy. It is good to note that your phone may have light settings you can activate that help reduce the screens effect on sleep later on.

Once when visiting some friends, we observed as they put their children to bed with a television and video to watch as they fell asleep. I literally gasped out loud unable to suppress my dismay at the idea of grooming one's children to this questionable life habit. When I tentatively voiced this opinion, it was really awkward. On the way home afterwards, we discussed our personal decision to not allow televisions in our kid's room and our regrettable losing battle with the night time phone usage during our kid's teen years. We know many families allow their children to have their own televisions and devices but it's honestly not a good idea. Instead, light soothing music is a better idea if you have children that need settling as they go to sleep.

Many people cultivate poor sleep habits that they get by with in their youth but as they age, those poor habits wreak havoc on their rest. I used to sleep very soundly but as most mothers do, I slept lightly, hearing every sound while my babies grew up. My husband slept with earplugs so I was the designated listener and I was good at it. I could hear a whimper and the precursors to vomiting in the dead of night.

I heard too much. Our home makes a variety of noises and so does our neighbourhood. I was constantly waking to one sound or another. Even after the children were grown and independent, my mother hearing did not stop and menopause symptoms added a new disruption. My new reality was that my best sleep hours were between 10pm and 3am. Somehow, I would always wake at 3am and it was fitful, light sleep after that. For a while I was plagued with anxiety dreams and nightmares. I think some of that was due to stress.

I look back at my deep sleep days of childhood and wonder. Our nighttime rest is taken for granted and trampled on until later in life we are doing everything from wearing earplugs, taking supplements and using noise cancellation fans to enjoy it.

I used to be able to push my boundaries but now if I skip those precious minutes, I literally become impaired in my ability to drive.

So, respect your sleep and establish your sleep rituals. Your older self will thank you. So long as you are using your time wisely and not sleeping beyond your needs, you are not being lazy.

Chapter Eighteen

Weekly Rest

"Thus, the heavens and the earth were finished,

and all the host of them.

And on the seventh day God ended his work which he had

made; and he rested on the seventh day

from all his work which he had made.

And God blessed the seventh day, and sanctified it:

because that in it he had rested from all his work

which God created and made."

Genesis 2:1-3 KJV

When I was a child, I hated naps. I think it was fear of missing out but I also hated the interruption of fun with a period of sequestering to a bedroom alone. Of course, I rarely slept. I used the oscillating fan as a microphone, studied the mesmerizing patterns of the wallpaper, looked enviously out the window at the neighbourhood kids playing outside, and waited for the interminable moment when I would be freed from the prison of quiet time.

For the most part I don't need naps even as an adult but when I was pregnant and my children were young, naps were vital. I needed them. I would try not to take them but I would get sucked in by the solace of the afternoon hours and an almost dizzying exhaustion that lulled me to unconsciousness.

The only difference between the me that hated naps and the me that relished them was the season of life which brought different physical, emotional and mental demands on my body.

I think the sabbath rest precipitated by God and legislated in the Ten Commandments is generally regarded the same way my young self deemed imposed nap time. No thank you! Too much to do! Businesses don't want to close. People push their limits with endless work or recreational pursuits.

It's not until you hit years of realizing your limits and the toll that a life void of proper rest can take that you can appreciate the blessing of this sacred example.

Rest is holy. Rest is replenishing.

I mentioned in my introduction that for a period of time I did my best to observe a weekly "Sabbath".

Not in a religious adherence to the mosaic law given to the Jews, but as a worshipful experiment. Could I accomplish all I had to do in my six workdays so that I would not be tempted to shop, clean or cook on Sunday? Could I really put aside all my projects and just "be" for an entire day that was bookended by communal church services?

I found value in fasting after dinner Saturday night (usually a feast-type meal with friends or family) until after prayer service Sunday night or Monday morning. This was because fasting made me a little tired and slowed me down. I took naps or sat quietly. My family ate reheated leftovers because I wasn't preparing food.

I had to cease fasting because I was doing too much of it and it was having an adverse effect but now that I've realigned my life and even changed my diet, I am considering a return to that discipline, albeit in a relaxed, non-religious, non-performance way. When the discipline doesn't serve to love ourselves or others around us, it is better to put it aside. I wouldn't want anyone to read this who has a performance mindset as I do and feel compelled to accomplish this goal at all costs.

If you have a family dinner to host or attend, eat! If you are hard pressed with negative side effects from going without food, eat! The main goal is for you to rest and be replenished as you put aside work and connect with those you love.

If you wish to fast but cannot, eat lightly. That is a rest too. Let go of the all or nothing mindset. While there are great things to gain by observing rituals of rest, there is no award or even final destination to tell you that you have achieved enough. That is why I am comfortable saying I once did this and now I do not.

Sabbath or weekly rest doesn't have to include fasting. It can be as simple as making extra food on Friday and Saturday so all you need to do is reheat. If you enjoy sandwiches prepared the day before, that is fine too.

The idea is to live life more simply and lightly, giving yourself permission to let the household tasks sit undone until the next day.

In my childhood, I read Laura Ingalls Wilder's "Little House on The Prairie" book series where I came upon a foreign-sounding Sunday observance in "Farmer Boy" and "The Big Woods". Laura describes how her husband, Almanzo Wilder, and his family spent their Sunday "Sabbath" sitting still in chairs gathered in a common room. No playing, laughing or talking. Just silence from the time they finished post service lunch until sundown. It sounded terrible! From Laura's description, Almanzo certainly didn't enjoy that ritual.[18]

On the other hand, today Sundays are often treated like any other day. A catch-up day. You can do almost anything on a

---

[18] Laura Ingalls Wilder's account of Almanzo's childhood Sunday "Sabbath"
https://faithofliw.wordpress.com/2016/01/15/farmer-boy/

Sunday albeit in more restrained business hours. Businesses like Chick-fil-a and Hobby Lobby that remain closed on Sundays are an oddity when it used to be the norm.

So, what should weekly rest look like for you? I can't dictate that. There is a gap between my own ideals and the reality I live out. I recommend reflection and discussion with your family as to how you should observe a day of rest in your week.

Hopefully, you find a way to spend that time with more joy than hours of silence in a straight-backed chair, with more reverence than an afternoon of shopping and more rest than a day filled with common chores.

I cover the concept of weekly rest in more detail later in the section on Spiritual Perspectives.

Chapter Nineteen

Vacations

Vacation! Isn't that such a happy word? It inspires dreams of a triumphant exit from the workplace, excitedly boarding a plane and disembarking at a heavenly, tropical destination. Beach, sun, fruity frozen beverages, clear blue waters. Or perhaps it means packing up to visit a beloved cabin or trailer "up north" where life is simpler, slower and more social. Vacation could mean packing up the car and driving to a campsite where the tent is pitched and the cooler is unloaded by a picnic table for a mostly outdoor adventure that involves spidery public bathrooms, campfires and night-time pillagers. Some opt for stay-cations where they enjoy the additional opportunity to enjoy the comforts of home, saving money, or getting an important project done that will make going back to work less burdensome.

Whatever your definition of vacation and your budget, I hope that how you spend your precious days and weeks off work bring lasting rest and replenishment. You should be able to return to work in a better state than you left, not more dependant on work than before. Over the years I've observed many families jeopardize their financial futures, homes and family relationships to enjoy vacations that they really couldn't afford. Their efforts to "escape" from their lives only leave them more stuck in the misery that they long to take a break from.

In my experience, this is most prevalent among those who love...do I dare say it? The biggest vacation budget busters I've ever met are...Disney enthusiasts. Eek! Yes, I just used the "D" word. It's not just Disney lovers though. There are lots of high-cost cruises and resort vacationers among my readers too. You know who you are. YOLO is your vacation creed!

I'm not here to make you feel bad or villainize you for aiming to have an awesome vacation. Maybe I'm even a little bit jealous because I've chosen a different path than you have and it would be nice to have both life results. We can just agree that neither of us is wrong, we are just different. I'm just going to share my opinions and experiences in case you aren't so happy with your vacation decisions and the resulting financial fallout. Maybe knowing that someone has tried a different strategy and didn't die from lack of cartoon vacation fun is all the encouragement you need to try something different.

Before I dive in, it's important to know that my husband and I have divided vacations into two categories: Commercial and Natural.

A commercial vacation would be amusement or water parks, cruise ships, organized city tours, shopping and any other event or destination that is stimulating, colourful, heavily marketed and fee-based. We've personally sampled Disney, Cedarpoint, Canada's Wonderland, Niagara Falls, water-park resorts, cruises and tours that fall into the "Commercial" category. There is a direct exchange of money for promised pleasure or experience. Glossy pamphlets, colourful websites and commercials all attempt to convince you that if you choose this particular entertainment experience, you will be euphorically happy.

This marketing is especially aimed at children and parents of children. Children see advertisement after advertisement promising excitement and adventure in cartoon colour that assures blissful happiness. Parents see commercials of other children being surprised with tickets to these special venues and they light up with delight and throw their arms around their benevolent, sacrificial parents with glee. It's not that these entertainment breaks aren't fun and enjoyable at all but it's rare that they play out like the marketing projects. There are lines, heat, bad moods, crowds, unexpected costs, injuries, physical limitations, closures, bad weather and all sorts of fun-disrupting elements that can detract from the promised experience and leave you wondering what all the hype was about.

A natural vacation is where you go out to nature in some way and you interact with the outdoors. Campgrounds, cabins, hiking, cycling, boating...are some examples. You set yourself up in a more outdoor-friendly accommodation and you leave time largely unstructured so everyone finds restful activities to enjoy.

Some of my favourite vacation memories as a child involve stopping at a roadside vendor for fresh fruits and veggies on our way to a cabin up north where we spend our days swimming in a lake, reading and exploring the forest. My favourite getaways with my own children were similar.

Natural vacations have detractors too. Rain, bugs, fire bans, extreme heat, trail closures, and complaints of boredom can make you wonder why you left the comfort of home at all.

It's important to know which vacation type makes you feel happy and rested but more importantly, why? What is it about your chosen vacation that fills you with joy? If you think about the elements of your vacation that make it special such as childhood nostalgia, sense of adventure, trying new things, etc., then you can begin to look at lower cost alternatives that achieve the same objective.

Cost isn't the only issue at stake. Often there is disparity between couples as to which kind of vacation fuels the other person. The cruelty of attraction is that a nature lover may be espoused to a commercial lover. The result is that one person is getting their way and being fuelled while the other is being dragged along and not getting what they need.

My husband and I experienced this for many years. We would do vacations that we both agreed on but both of us longed for the vacations that the other person had vetoed during the selection process. Neither of us wanted to become the couple that vacationed separately but attempts to drag each other on a getaway of the other person's preference were disastrous.

A few years ago, I introduced a vacation concept that felt almost wrong to us initially but has become incredibly successful. At the time we had three weeks of vacation a year. After a very refreshing week visiting a school-friend...a trip that my husband would not have enjoyed at all...I suggested that we try the following vacation routine:

Winter-Take a sunny vacation together as a couple. We both like sun, warmth, beaches and sleep. This is a mutually enjoyable vacation.

Summer-Take a vacation as a family. This could be commercial or natural but the goal is family time.

Autumn-Take individual discretionary vacations. My husband likes to go on a week-long motorcycle getaway with other men and I gravitate to reflective, meditative vacations with other women. Neither of us would enjoy spending a week on the vacations of the other person's choice.

After four years, I can tell you that this is one of the best things we have done for our marriage. That week is a tribute to the activities that replenish us as individuals and have contributed more to our personal enjoyment and growth than could be imagined. I wouldn't be sitting here writing this book if I hadn't discovered this vacation strategy.

"Love me, love my vacation style" causes a lot of misery between couples. Everyone needs some opportunity to do the relaxation activities that fuel their personal life passion without another person sabotaging or detracting from the experience in some way. Don't take it too far though. Couples need SHARED relaxation experiences too and it's important to learn how to spend a vacation where fair negotiation and compromise take place. We need both.

In the case of many of my "D"-loving friends, one spouse was typically gung-ho to spend the family fortune or credit to do all the "things" and the other was not. A few couples took us into their confidence but when we advised against the trip in favour of a more practical use of their money, the trip commenced and the financial advice-asking stopped. "D" is the holy grail of vacations and we had dared to challenge that and could no longer be trusted. Smile. While I understand that they are perfectly entitled to make their own choices, I don't personally connect with the appeal. I wouldn't trade our current financial position for any number of trips to "D". I should quantify though that my trips to "D" were on a budget. I've never experienced staying on the resort and all the luxury that that would entail so maybe I'm ill-informed and just don't know better.

The important thing to take from this chapter is that it's important that your vacations fuel your joy, rest and replenishment but don't syphon your family budget. Next to homes, vehicles and dining out, vacations can be a major expense that only serves to tether you more firmly to a long lifetime of working beyond your ideal capacities.

Chapter Twenty

Out of Emergency Mode

One may ask about sabbaticals, "Why the need for such a long rest? Wouldn't a series of smaller breaks be just as good?" I've asked myself the same thing and come to realize something about me that is probably true for many.

When life is going at a fast pace, I go into what I call "emergency mode".

It means I am mentally calculating the various demands and deadlines and how I am going to manage them. My breath is shallower. My brow is furrowed. My voice is more clipped. The moment one task is done, I'm on to the next. Niceties, casual conversation and laughter pretty much disappear. I'm generally annoyed by the sound of anyone having fun or talking about vacation.

My husband exhibits the same symptoms when he is in what I call "work mode". He is a completely different person than the man I experience when he is relaxed.

This is fairly normal except for some it is harder to snap out of "emergency" or "work" mode when it goes on for extended periods of time or if it becomes part of your identity as a person.

It is also hard to snap out of hyperdrive during short reprieves because a short vacation can tend to cause extra work on the front-end preparation and back-end from clean-up. If not careful, the "rest" or vacation itself can get too hectic and stressful with excess activities that leave one in a worse state of stress than before.

In fact, for me, vacations can be particularly challenging depending on the circumstances. The hustle and bustle of preparing and travel can wreak havoc on my digestive system and sex drive. This is because the human body is not meant to procreate in times of stress and elimination is either sped up or avoided completely to allow for fight or flight.[19]

I cannot emphasize how many times a vacation has ADDED to my sense of emergency instead of eased it. After years of misadventures I am learning what I need to tap into true rest and relaxation.

The longer the rest, the more deeply you are able to unwind and distance yourself from the realities that caused the winding in the first place. The stomach unclenches. The sense of retribution for lapses of enjoyment lessens. You can stop to observe what's going on around you. You can put down the phone and be okay with missing a call or text while you go for a walk.

Life takes on that timeless sensation you experienced as a child during summer vacation where time is measured not by the clock, alarms and deadlines but by sunrises, hunger, happy

---

[19] Read more about stress effects on the body: https://theconversation.com/what-happens-to-your-body-when-youre-stressed-81789?xid=PS_smithsonian

experiences, environmental sounds and sunsets. For a while, you can enjoy a sense of elevation from the constant clicking of a clock. It's like flying, really.

We used to camp when the kids were young and as you can imagine, the preparations were massive, plus the work of meal preparation as well as keeping ourselves AND the tent camper clean were extensive. I remember saying to my husband that it wasn't worth all the work unless we camped for two consecutive weeks in one location.

It's fairly standard for Europeans to take month long holidays.

Longer vacations really do allow you to decompress better.

It's not enough to take a roomy vacation. You must be aware of who you are sharing that time with and ensure that you will be able to get the rest you need. I like a good adventure as much as the next person but lately I've been gravitating to trips that, to some, would seem boring.

The past couple years I've used a week vacation to visit the International House of Prayer. There is around 20 hours of teaching but there is a delicious 20 hours in the prayer room listening to worship music, praying, and journaling.

This year I have booked a week at a neighbouring city's university to indulge in a self-guided writing retreat. The week will be peppered with writing time, nature walks, bike rides and stretching.

In the past we took a cruise vacation. My parents had generously treated all of us to an amazing trip. A few days in I had to put the brakes on. We had done two excursions and a lot of travel and it wasn't looking to ease up. I had the wisdom to set my boundaries even though it meant breaking from what everyone else was doing. Instead of getting up at dawn for a quick breakfast so I could exit our ship at the next two ports, I slept in. Instead of dressing and getting ready immediately to go for breakfast in the dining room, I ordered coffee and fruit to my cabin where I listened to audio-books and knitted. I took advantage of the emptier ship to have a quiet lunch devoid of the long lines that usually prevailed. I worked out at the ship gym and enjoyed the spa's sauna and hot tub. Later, rested and happy, I listened to everyone else's adventures during dinner. It was perfect.

How different it would've been if I had betrayed my need for rest to lose sleep and sanity shopping with my parents or looking for adventure with my husband and tweens. I still remember that trip with fondness...even the busier days at the start because I had recognized my limits and voiced them in enough time to balance the trip experience. Instead of dismissing cruising as too busy, I simply modified it to fit my needs.

Another fabulous trip my husband and I enjoyed was to Cuba. We literally checked into our hotel and laid out in cabana loungers on the beach everyday except two. We took a bus tour and explored a local market. We barely swam. We didn't do sports or games. We slept and ate and, on that trip, I read an actual hard cover book from the hotel library (I HATED the ending) and played candy crush on my phone with zero recrimination. It was exactly what we needed.

The absolutely worst trip I ever took in terms of physical rest was to Israel. Before I explain why, I want to emphasize that this was a trip of a lifetime that I am very grateful for and highly recommend that every person take if you can. Just don't have the expectation of a restful experience.

While I was enthusiastic about the culture, history and spiritual significance of the journey, I was overwhelmed by the demands of overseas travel, rigid touring schedules, multiple hotel changes and the number of people we interacted with every day. I was alternating between elation and crises most of the trip.

When we returned, I went straight back to work exhausted and with mixed feelings. Later it was suggested that we follow that week with a restful vacation but I had scheduled my vacation slots for the year and there was no room for a decompression time.

Again, if you desire to visit the Holy Land, this is not meant to dissuade you but to set your expectations and encourage you to plan rest accordingly following your trip.

So, choose as long of a vacation or break as your time and budget will allow. Share your rest with like-minded people or with people who will respect your relaxation needs. Be judicious with your rest activities. Simpler, low key plans are recommended.

My hope for you is that you will come out of "emergency" or "work" mode long enough to relax at a cellular and limbic level so you can return to work refreshed and ready to give your best.

Chapter Twenty-One

Seven Year Rest

While daily, weekly and vacation rest may be familiar to most of us, the concept of a sabbatical is less common. The idea of an extended period of time away from job responsibilities in order to rest is almost unheard of today in most circles.

The two professions that have embraced the sabbatical in the past are the clergy and professorships. I personally know two ministers who have taken sabbaticals but undoubtedly there are more. Having said that, it is becoming less and less heard of in modern times.

Many of these professionals take the time to cultivate their own spirituality and education, often completing a writing project related to their lifetime work.

Some seekers and creatives take sabbaticals from work to travel and experience inspiration from other cultures.

If you have never heard of a sabbatical before you may be surprised to learn that its origin began with the Mosaic law recorded in Leviticus (an early chapter in the Bible).

If you went to Sunday school you may be familiar with the story of Moses. He was rescued by an Egyptian princess from the Nile river and raised in the palace until he killed an Egyptian. He then fled to the desert. Later, after an experience with a talking, burning bush, he led the children of Israel out of slavery from the Egyptians and into the desert toward their promised land.

En route, he stopped and went up a mountain where God officially wrote a set of community laws and rules that would define His people from other nations. That is where we get the Ten Commandments and many other basics that contribute to our legal system even to this day.

Among all those important guidelines that Moses was given, God thought it important enough to include some parameters around work to allow for rest. Not only did these instructions talk about weekly rest (Sabbath Day), but they also included year-long rests to be observed every seven years.

"Wherefore ye shall do my statutes, and keep my judgments,

and do them; and ye shall dwell in the land in safety.

And the land shall yield her fruit, and ye shall eat your fill,

and dwell therein in safety.

And if ye shall say, what shall we eat the seventh year?

behold, we shall not sow, nor gather in our increase:

Then I will command my blessing upon you in the sixth year,

and it shall bring forth fruit for three years.

And ye shall sow the eighth year, and eat yet of old fruit until the

ninth year; until her fruits come in ye shall eat of the old store."

Leviticus 25:18-22 KJV

What makes this passage so wondrous to me is that God inserted these commands to rest among passages that address sexuality, worship, property, justice, and other very serious topics. It was as though God took the balance between work and rest as seriously as every other issue.

God's command to let the land rest every seven years is indicative of a supreme creator who is concerned not only with man's wellbeing but also the care and sustainability of the Earth He had provided him to manage.

It doesn't stop with the command to stop farming. God then gives assurance that if His word is observed, the crop harvested on year six would be enough to last three years! Wow! What an amazing promise!

As with all promises that God has made, there is a certain level of faith that is needed. I mean, could you imagine the step of faith needed to be taken by a farmer to simply not plow and sow on the seventh year? You hope your baskets of produce and canned goods will see you through not only to the next harvest but the one after that!

It sounds like such a lovely idea but can you imagine actually TRUSTING God to keep His word while your farmer neighbours whisper behind your back about your laziness and idealism? Would you not be seized with doubting thoughts and wonder if you are a fool? What if you and your family starve and everyone shakes their heads at your misfortune?

I would say that taking God at His word in that capacity would've been so brave! Unbelievably brave.

While the Jewish family rested from the work of agriculture, so did the land. The cycle of working and resting was supposed to make the crops abundant and, I imagine, give a glimmer of hope to the backbreaking labour of farming. Perhaps they found other creative things to do with the time they usually spent in crop cultivation

I'm not Jewish and I don't grow crops for a living. Neither is there anything in this text that commands a Gentile in the 21st century to quit their job every seventh year to rest. It's just that it inspired me to start studying sabbaticals and the possible value of taking extended rest from work in our modern world.

My search brought me to a few videos of people describing their sabbatical years and the renewed creativity and perspective it gave them. A lot of people travel during their sabbatical year. I was amazed at their separation from the standard routine of life. Their pause on the accumulation of material possessions. Their amazing tales of revitalization and innovation as a result.

Could there be something to this ancient life cycle that unleashes a powerful principle of trust and promise that gives birth to newness of life?

I had to find out for myself.

I should mention that the Jewish people didn't necessarily follow this instruction. When they were taken into Babylonian captivity for 70 years, the Bible reads that the land finally got the rest that had been neglected. Wow. 70 Sabbath years that had not been taken no doubt out of mistrust, greed, and fear.

Even if that sixth-year harvest was abundant enough to last three years, did the people think of slowing down to rest or were they driven to produce more and more. Maybe some did and others didn't and the ones who pressed unrelentingly in their farming looked so much better for it that the ones who rested abandoned their worshipful observance.

I cannot speak for the Israelites but I can say that in choosing to pause my work to rest, I feel completely at odds with society norms. I haven't determined what the end of this period will look like but I feel as though I could easily brave another six years of work if I knew I would have another season of reprieve to look forward to.

Chapter Twenty-Two

A New Model

I had the joy of watching a TedTalk called "The Power of Time Off"[20] in which the speaker, Stefan Sagmeister, shared how every seven years, he closes his New York design studio for a year-long sabbatical to rejuvenate and refresh his team's creative outlook.

During his talk he suggests a tweaking of our North American working model. The idea is that most of us set out in our lifetimes to work all our adult years from age 19-65 in order to enjoy retirement after that. It is a long period of delayed gratification and often one's health and quality of life is compromised by the time the retirement period begins.

---

[20] Watch Stefan Sagmeister's TedTalk:
https://www.ted.com/talks/stefan_sagmeister_the_power_of_time_off?language=en

Instead, it's suggested that you take a number of your retirement years and intersperse them in your working years as sabbaticals. You may have to work later in life but you will have enjoyed soul replenishing reprieves that allow you to reflect on your life choices. You will also have used some of your vital years to do activities you may not be able to do in your aged season of life.

It is a periodic reconnecting with yourself to ensure that the person who celebrates retirement arrives there intact and emotionally healthy because you have the opportunity to keep recalibrating your life as needed over the years. You will have the assurance that you sailed the course to your intended destination.

In Stefan's case, that year sabbatical is critical to his life's work as it allows him to work on creative projects that fuel his skill as a designer.

I was captivated by this idea of reshuffling a number of our retirement years into our working ones and opting to retire later. How many healthy 65-year-olds are forced out of the workplace simply because of their age? How many men drive their wives crazy and feel loss of purpose because they never cultivated a life outside of work and then suddenly find that their life purpose has simply disappeared? How many people never get to experience joy and freedom during their best years only to perish before they reach retirement?

I love how provisions have been made for parental leave after the birth of a child. It is lovely how a person's position is saved for them while they enjoy time with their new child and all the demands of care. I would advocate that similar provisions should be made to those who work a certain length of time, so they could enjoy a reprieve without fear of losing their job.

Having said that, I don't think we should wait until the government requires companies to facilitate sabbaticals. The smart planner and budgeter with an adventurous spirit can make this happen for themselves if they want to. It just requires that we look at life differently and adjust our values.

Contemplation of Part V

1. Have you ever found yourself trying to accomplish something out of season? If so, please explain.

2. Have you experienced the ending of one season and the beginning of another (transition)? If so, what was the difficult part and what was the blessing?

3. Do you allow for at least an hour of daily rest so you can do something relaxing and pleasurable each day? If so, please explain.

4. Do you practise healthful sleep habits? List your positive habits versus your negative ones. Where are you doing well and where can you improve?

5. Do you ever feel guilty for getting adequate sleep? If so, what belief system is driving that guilt?

6. Do you practise a day of rest every week? If so, how do you do so? What does it look like? Is it purposeful or incidental?

7. Does God's command to rest once a week make you feel happy or confined? Why?

8. Have you noticed a shift in your attitude toward rest over your lifetime in one way or the other?

9. Could you become more purposeful in observing weekly rest without becoming religious or rigid? Why?

10. How do you feel about businesses that opt to be closed one day a week to observe rest when most businesses opt to be open?

11. Do you think you could begin to trust God with your time and finances enough to give a measure to Him in obedience to rest?

12. Do you take regular vacations? If so, do you prefer commercial or natural vacations? Why?

13. Do you have a voice in how you spend your vacation time? If not, how would you change what you do?

14. What did you think of Shawn and Melissa's vacation strategy? Have you tried something similar in your family?

15. Have you ever had to put boundaries down during a vacation when you felt it was getting too busy? If so, please explain.

16. Do you feel rested and refreshed after vacation? If not, what changes need to be made to make that happen?

17. How do you feel about the amount of money you spend on your vacations and do you think you could accept a lower cost vacation if it meant you didn't have to work so much year-round?

18. How long are your vacations? Do you feel like you get out of "emergency mode" and truly relax in that window of time?

19. Make a list of relaxing, lower cost vacations that you could enjoy either with your spouse, family or alone.

20. Are you surprised at God's command to the Israelites to rest from farming every seven years? Why do you think He wanted them to do that?

21. Do you think that ancient command is still important to God today? Why or why not?

22. Considering that the Bible reports that the Israelites were not obedient to the practise of taking sabbaticals from farming, why do you think they didn't?

23. If God was commanding YOU to stop all work every seven years and TRUST Him to provide for you, could you do that? Why or why not?

24. Have you ever taken a sabbatical or heard of someone who did? If so, how did it change your or their life?

25. What do you think about the idea of interspersing sabbatical years into the adult working life and retiring from work later?

26. How do you think your life would be different if you had regular year-long breaks from work every seven years?

27. Would it be possible for you to change the rhythm of your life to that degree without major disaster? How would it change your priorities and goals?

Notes

Part VI: Getting Finances in Order

Chapter Twenty-Three

Mastering Your Money

As I think about our life together, I realize that Shawn and I started planting seeds for this journey of rest and sustainable living many years ago when we acknowledged our need to take control of our finances. We were existing as many people do...in debt living pay-cheque to pay-cheque. We were continuously spending more money every month than we made.

This caused tremendous frustration for us because we thought we were intelligent and successful people, yet the balancing of our income and spending was always eluding us. It caused a lot of grief in our marriage.

It wasn't until we listened to an audio copy of Dave Ramsey's "*The Total Money Makeover*[21]" that we found a practical, if not radical approach to debt-reduction and money management that we could understand and practise.

We were very zealous and focused. We were rewarded for our efforts (with a lot of help from a series of miracles) by being debt free in less than two years. We even had an emergency fund and savings for retirement! We've moderated our approach a bit but we still follow the budgeting and spending techniques that we learned all those years ago. We are blessed to be a few years away from paying off the mortgage and the future looks bright!

We facilitated Dave Ramsey's "*Financial Peace University*" classes at our church for a time and I watched people struggle with the sacrifices required to regain control of their finances. Gym memberships, Disney trips and various lessons for the kids...these were some of the things that they simply could not trade for financial freedom.

---

[21] Learn more about The Total Money Makeover: https://amzn.to/33UkT5I

I'm not here to condemn anyone's spending choices. Even on a budget there is tremendous freedom to open your wallet for what you prefer and value. It's just that unless you can gain control of yourself and your spending habits, you will always be a slave to work.

Work is a wonderful thing. We need to work and be productive to fully enjoy the beauty of rest. Being a slave to work is different. You are not in control when you are a slave. Deciding from a place of power as you manage the pendulum of work and rest is completely different than slaving for a pay-cheque that barely covers your expenses.

Even people who make a generous wage find that they spend as quick as they earn. When we are broke, we think a larger income will fix our situation, however when you are making more money, it is typical to become accustomed to a more expensive way of life. The result is that you quickly find yourself in the same "broke" circumstances, only in a higher tax category.

Out of control spending and debt snuffs hope and joy from your life. You sink deeper and deeper into the pit of despair and bad financial choices because it doesn't seem to matter anymore what you do.

I'm here to tell you that it's not too late! If you get some good material and make the hard choices you will experience hope and freedom in your heart first. If you stay the course, you will experience a better financial life than you currently have.

We made a lot of hard choices. We sold precious belongings that we didn't want to let go of. We went without pleasures that others were enjoying. We didn't give our children as much as was in our hearts to give. Now, years later, I am so grateful for those painful sacrifices!

We are fans of Dave Ramsey because his materials were our guide out of financial distress but there are others. What you want is a program that encourages you to stop borrowing, provides a realistic budget approach and a plan to repay your debts, along with a savings strategy for emergencies, large purchases, and retirement.

We have no experience with this but I don't like the programs that consolidate all your debts and put you on a payment plan that they manage. Perhaps this is a legitimate option for certain situations but my concern is that it doesn't teach the discipline and skills needed to change behaviours permanently. Worst case scenario is that you are adding expense to your debt to pay the third party and/or you are being scammed. This is something to consider when being enticed by promises of painless debt-repayment. Easier does not always mean better.

Chapter Twenty-Four

Practical Tips to Fund Your Dreams

One cannot responsibly preach a message of slowing down, rest and sabbaticals...living the life you've always dreamed of...without addressing the hard reality of finances. A more reasonable balance between work and play sounds romantic and enviable until the bills pile up and the car breaks down. Still, there is a path one can proactively walk that will lead to having means to fund your dreams on some level, whatever those dreams may be.

What is the end goal?

A speaker at our church told a story written by German writer, Heinrich Boll, that had a huge impact on me and has become increasingly clear as our family-raising life stage ended and empty nest stage has begun. Here is the abbreviated version:

A businessman meets a laid-back Mexican fisherman on the beach and encourages him to take the initiative to build a fishing boat empire (explaining the multiple steps to success). When the fisherman questions what the final objective of all that labour is, it turns out to be an elaborate plan to enjoy the life that he is already enjoying.[22]

We see this play out in our communities as individuals work for homes that are bigger and better, filling them with lots of stuff only to "downsize" later in life to a home that requires getting rid of all their accumulated possessions.

We can't have everything.

I'm not against building businesses or buying big homes and collecting some quality material goods...I've just learned that life is about choices. When we choose one thing, we are NOT choosing something else. There's a lie that makes us think it's

---

[22] Read entire Mexican fisherman story: https://www.becomingminimalist.com/recognizing-happiness/

possible to have it all. That's completely false. Some people's choices are more limited than others but we all have some measure of decision to make.

My husband and I have made choices in home ownership, spending and saving that will allow us to own our home mortgage-free in a few years. We are so excited! We have a choice. We can be content with our home and neighbourhood and enjoy the time and financial freedom that comes with being mortgage-free...Or, instead, we can sell our home and take the full amount as a down-payment on a bigger one on the waterfront and work another 20 plus years to enjoy the financial space we are currently in.

We decided that unless some windfall of money comes our way, we're going to stick with dream A. That's a choice. We want both but we have to choose.

Debt is Enemy #1

I can't stress this enough. If I could wave a magic wand and go back 28 years, I would jump in front of the Sears credit card sign-up table and tell my college-student self to put down the pen. Instead, I saw the obtaining of a credit card as a rite of passage to adulthood. It had a $500 limit but I soon realized how quickly $500 is spent and how heavy a $500 debt feels. I managed to pay it off but when my husband and I married, we consistently used loans and credit cards in a buy now, pay later mentality to fund our lifestyle. We were both working and living what we felt was a necessity-based lifestyle and yet, we were consistently spending more than we made and getting deeper into debt every month.

We didn't have control over debt. Fortunately, through a series of events, we were introduced to a debt reduction/financial freedom program that taught us how to get out of debt, save for the future and spend responsibly. That program saved our marriage and ultimately our lives. I'm forever grateful for the discipline of money management even though I chafe at it even now.

During the early years of that program, we couldn't use a credit card at all. Now we have a few for various purposes, but you know what? We know our limits. We pay the credit cards off monthly and only borrow occasionally to do a project or buy a large-ticket item and then focus on paying that one item off. We approach debt cautiously and soberly because neither of us wants to go back to where we were.

There are times where debt is necessary, but our society has gotten that skewed out of control. For most of us it's not about medical bills or keeping our families off the street...its about upgrading to the latest phone or having a night out at a fancy restaurant. I like those things as much as anyone else. It's just that, once you taste the amazing sensation of being debt-free, you can't give that up so easily for things that don't really matter.

New Management

Just today my husband and I were separately going about our respective chores after accounting for this month and setting our budget for the next. Since I haven't been making an income for the past seven months, there wasn't a whole lot to spread around and we were verbally reflecting on that.

Sometimes we can focus only on what we need to improve and not give credit for what we are rocking at. I'm going to list some of the ways we manage our money that may or may not be typical but definitely allow us to focus on what is important:

- We write up a budget every month. It's based on our regular monthly income only. Any extra income is allotted to savings or special purchases but we do not count on it for our basic living costs.

- We use a money accounting program. For us it's "You Need a Budget[23]" (YNAB). It's a bit complicated to learn but it ties together your bank accounts and your budget so that you know exactly where you are in each category at all times.

- We sit down to update YNAB once a week, go through receipts, download transactions, update the budget. We could keep it up on our phones as we do transactions but neither of us have mastered that level of discipline.

- We follow up on overcharges, unpaid rewards, warranties, store returns, rebates, and subscription

---

[23] Learn more about YNAB:
https://www.youneedabudget.com/

renewals to keep our bank account hemorrhaging to a minimum.

- We use points and rewards programs strategically. If you are in debt, don't play this game. When you are the master of your money, you can have a little fun. If a rewards program tempts you to buy what you otherwise would not, don't do it. Choose programs that coincide with your regular or preferred purchasing habits.

Our favourite is the Costco Capital One Mastercard Gold Cash Rewards program along with Costco's own Executive Membership rewards. We pay a nominal amount for our annual membership but the rewards we get back twice a year not only cover that membership but can be refunded to us in CASH at the register. Most other rewards come in the form of points that have limited use. Since we don't carry a balance or pay interest of any kind, we make money on purchases we would make anyway.

- When we are finished with our possessions, we try to sell anything that has value on Facebook marketplace, Kijiji (Canada's equivalent to Craig's List in the US) or eBay.

Usually we look up what we paid versus what it is currently selling for and list at 40% less and expect 60% in the end after negotiations. (Example: A Fitbit that we paid $99 for but is now selling for $89 would be listed at $55 and we would accept $45.) This minimizes our loss and often helps fund new purchases. We take great care of our stuff so our buyers are very happy with what they get for their money.

- We try to time purchases with major sales events where pricing is lower than usual. It's not uncommon to delay purchases to Boxing Day, Black Friday, Cyber Monday and Small Business Tuesday-related promos.

- We minimize eating out by prepping and packaging our meals at home. Dinner leftovers are divided into single serving containers and stacked in the fridge and freezer for easy, convenient lunch grabs. Fruit and other snacks are portioned and packaged in easy-to-grab containers. Salads are arranged with homemade dressing in a mason jar in such a way as to keep it fresh until shaken and eaten on the go. All these measures create our own "fast food" which cut down on unplanned, hunger-driven drive-thru and restaurant visits. This happens to be great for health, too!

- Instead of expensive restaurant visits to celebrate special occasions, we sometimes opt to buy premium groceries and prepare a meal at home. Even a more expensive cut of meat and a few gourmet ingredients add up to far less than a typical restaurant meal and tip.

- Similar to above, we aim to entertain our friends in our home instead of treating them to dinner out. We can put out a very nice meal for far less than picking up a restaurant tab.

- We brew our own specialty drinks at home and take them with us. We own a Keurig and have some K-cups for convenience and company but on a daily basis we use refillable my-cup containers to brew our own signature blends. I like a particular decaf espresso blend with only one tsp of regular caffeinated espresso grinds added. Not only do I get exactly the amount of caffeine I can handle and the taste I love but it costs significantly less than a cafe visit. I still buy beverages at a cafe when I meet friends but that is way less often than my twice-a-day habit. Shawn has his own preferences but we both use the same brewing machine method.

- Repair broken goods instead of replacing them if at all possible. I realize that we are blessed as my husband can fix just about anything. He buys obscure parts from Amazon and our local parts stores and revives most of our stuff. When something breaks...everything from my costume jewelry, our son's RC or mowing equipment, our appliances, vehicles or anything else...it goes on Shawn's list and he revives it. Not everyone has this gift but most everyone has the capacity to do a little Internet searching and give repairs a go before calling it quits (don't tinker with stuff still under warranty). You can learn how do almost any repair by watching a YouTube video. Just give it a go before pitching and buying new.

- Embrace minimalism. A lot of people think that minimalism means you can't own much of anything and fail to realize that there is no one set standard for the minimalist lifestyle. Some minimalists keep their wardrobe items under a certain number and keep a kitchen on par with what could be found in a holiday rental kitchenette. Others, just moderate their lifestyles to avoid purchasing excess...whatever excess means to them.

Even though I like retail therapy as much as the next girl, I embrace minimalism as much as I can. Most minimalists share that they exchange quantity with quality. Instead of a bunch of cheap, fad items, they may opt for a single more expensive, quality, classic item.

It's about mindset really. Instead of purchasing on a whim with a buy-as-much-as-possible attitude, think about why you want to buy something, how it will be used, where you will need to store it, etc. and try to bring as little home as possible. I even say no to free stuff all the time because, in my mind, the stress of clutter is far, far too expensive.

- Embrace Marie Kondo's "The Life-Changing Magic of Tidying Up: The Japanese Art of Decluttering and Organizing[24]" method as it ties into minimalism. When purging your clutter, Marie suggests you hold every item you have in your hands and ask yourself if it sparks joy. If it does, keep it. If it doesn't, toss it out. Why not do that before purchasing? Set aside a product's newness and the marketing hype in the moment. Will this item add value to your life long-term or will it become a burden adding to the clutter? A few honest moments of contemplation before hitting the cash register can enable you to leave a purchase behind with no regrets.

- Clean and Maintain. A big part of wanting to purchase things is that we want the "newness" and "freshness" that looks better than what we currently have. I'm a big fan of that feeling too. What I have learned is that most of the time, that look can be attained by cleaning and maintaining

---

[24] Learn more about The Life-Changing Magic of Tidying Up: The Japanese Art of Decluttering and Organizing https://amzn.to/2TU4k5z

what I already own. We learned this when we would prepare something to sell. After a bit of elbow grease, Shawn and I would look at an item we were selling and wonder why we didn't invest the time in cleaning it up for ourselves while we had owned it.

One example of this is my purses. I love the look of the store purses sitting upright on the display shelves all perky and bright. I discovered that I could take the deflated, neglected purses on my closet floor, shake them out, wipe them off and stuff them with tissue or bubble wrap and achieve the same result! Now all my purses sit on display on a closet shelf just waiting to be chosen to go with an outfit. I have purses that have been around for years and am only occasionally tempted to buy a new one...but only if I'm willing to part with an old one in exchange.

Shoes? Before buying new ones, I give the ones I have a little TLC. I've wiped, used matching colour nail polish on heel nicks, crazy glued and replaced heel tips and runner laces. Any extra mileage a pair of shoes can give is great. The exception to this is if your shoes are actually causing you bodily damage and not supporting you properly. Footwear designed for physical activity should be quality and replaced as needed.

- Think long term expense. That amazing printer deal that the store is practically giving away? What do the print cartridges cost? That cool coffee brewer that is on sale? How much do the coffee pods cost and how many will you consume? That vehicle that will make you look like a cool cat? What is the gas mileage? That free, latest model phone? What is the monthly contract going to cost you? The dream pool or jacuzzi you desire? How much will it add to your monthly energy costs? Maybe paying a little more up front will save you more later. Take the time to consider all your options. If you do the numbers and you decide to go ahead knowing exactly what you are signing up for, then at least you made an educated choice.

- Become Marketing Savvy. The marketing of a product or service is a very calculated skill. There are very specific, proven methods that if implemented properly, will compel people to buy out of emotion. I'm not here to demonize marketing but my husband and I have become adept at recognizing the pull of marketing and learned how to get out of its gravitational pull long enough to make rational, logical choices instead. For me it's as easy as recognizing the emotional connection building and talking about it with my ever-pragmatic husband. It's important to have someone in your life who knows what you really want and can talk you out of making a detour you will regret.

Some signs that signal that marketing is sucking you in? Promises that a product will solve all your problems. Extra bonus items if you buy immediately instead of waiting. Limited time to buy or it will be gone. Prices are going to be raised if you don't get it this time around. Everyone else is doing it. (Fear of missing out — FOMO). You cannot succeed without this purchase.

If you hear this kind of language and feel yourself responding to it, pull back and evaluate what is going on. It doesn't necessarily mean you are being cheated...it just means you are making decisions emotionally, not logically, and you need to take heed.

There are many other practical things we do to maximize our budget to enjoy our lifestyle of choice. These are just a few.

So, remember to think carefully about the life you truly want to live and put aside the things that would take you away from that end. Avoid or get out of debt. Minimize convenience or restaurant foods. Make your own "takeout". Manage your belongings. Adopt a minimalistic mindset. Your budget will thank you.

Chapter Twenty-Five

Side Hustle: Good, Bad and Ugly

I know many lovely, healthy and productive people who wear a lot of hats. They buzz around in a flurry of activity that makes me wonder where they get their energy and stamina. I've even been one of those people during different seasons of my life.

Apart from the usual responsibilities of home, work, family and community they have side hustles. Additional business activity to add to the income of their main employment.

In the past, it was more common for a person to choose one source of income for their lifetime but in today's job market, that is uncommon. People are likely to change jobs several times or more in their lifetimes. It is extremely common for those same individuals to have side businesses to help bolster their incomes.

I have a word of caution from my years of experience with this. Beware the sectioning of yourself into more and more pieces. You are not adding, you are dividing. Those pockets of time that you give to your side hustle are not free, they come at a cost.

If you must be involved in extra activities of any kind, be sure to prioritize and express those boundaries clearly. I have an essential oil hobby that I have strict time and money boundaries on. I have no desire to build a multi-level marketing empire. It's not my passion. I just love essential oils and share them with others in a minimalistic way.

There are opportunities, bonuses, special gifts and other perks that I leave on the table due to my "lack of ambition" to "work my side biz" but I consciously make that choice because that's not where I want to spend all my energies. I give what is convenient and authentic to my every day life and leave the rest. This is not to say I'm sloppy with my fulfilment of commitments. It's more of a cautious and realistic setting of people's expectations of what I can honestly deliver.

I'm not against setting up different income streams. I think the person who can create multiple sources of residual income is extremely brilliant and to be envied. To be honest, I'm doing so myself even now. I'm just more interested in setting up PASSIVE income streams...the make money while you sleep type and not ACTIVE ones.

If you are considering setting up a passive income stream it often requires some resources up front and a level of maintenance to harvest your returns. A relative of mine teaches by day (active income) and owns a rental home (passive income). She had to invest the capital to buy the home and even though, for the most part, she earns from the monthly rent she brings in, she still has to interview new renters, contract maintenance on the home, and do the books.

Counting the cost of your time and money is important and so is having realistic expectation of earnings. There are a lot of wonderful people who invest vital resources in ventures that promise the sun, moon and stars by those who are marketing it. The risks and work beyond the initial investment are minimized and rewards are maximized in an attempt to make it look easy and effortless.

I would encourage people to choose their life divides judiciously and weigh the pros and cons intensely before committing to multiple paths. Often the intangibles are what slip through the cracks of an overly divided life. You may wake up one day to find that you never made that promised fortune and that no-one in your life is happy with the slivers of time you have to offer. You may realize that you divided yourself in pieces so small that there is no substance to you anymore. You've become an appetizer not a main dish.

Most of all, if you are not staying as whole as possible for the most important portions of life, you may find you are not enough for YOU either.

If you find yourself in this predicament you may want to schedule a day or two to sit down and reflect on how you are spending your time, money and energy. Is there anything in your life that is not giving back? Are there some materialistic benefits that you could let go of that would allow you to reclaim more of yourself?

A good exercise is to picture yourself in a crisis that requires you to leave your home with only what you could carry. Everything else would have to be left behind to be enjoyed by others and you would never see it again. You and you alone would bear the weight of what you decided to take with you. What would you bring? What would you leave behind?

I'm a heavy packer so this exercise is tough for me. I like planning for every contingency and bringing along my personal comforts. Every once in a while, I like to go minimalistic and try to fit everything into a purse and carry-on. Wow, is that ever hard.

Some of us just like our "stuff" and we twist ourselves into pretzels doing all sorts of craziness to get more and more of it. That's why it's important to remember that we can't take ANY of it with us when we die. We work our entire lifetimes to accumulate things that will either be sold or taken and enjoyed by others.

Hold your possessions loosely and guard the resources you use to possess them. When is enough, enough?

Chapter Twenty-Six

Buyer Beware

Just as I entered the vulnerable expanse of time that my sabbatical allowed, my inspiration and dreaming came alive. I pondered my desire to write a book and the message that I wanted to share with the world. Just the same, I had no idea how to make it happen. I remember praying for God to show me how to go about this while making our bed one morning.

Within a few days I received an email from a writer I subscribe to inviting me to a free, online writing conference by *Flourish Writers*[25]! It was perfect! My budget wouldn't allow for travel or paying exorbitant fees for conferences or classes so

---

[25] Learn more about Flourish Writer's conference:
https://www.flourishwritersconference.com/welcome

something free and accessible from home was just what I needed! I wasn't sure how much help this conference would be but it was a step toward my goal and possibly I could learn something, anything to help me along.

I signed up and immediately was given an invitation to upgrade to lifetime access. It was tempting but because of my financial constraints, I declined. The emails started arriving with links to the video series with access for a limited time. I listened to every video made by published authors, editors, publishers, and marketers with fascinated enthusiasm. This was EXACTLY what I needed! So many questions I had about writing, publishing and marketing were answered in that beautiful collection of wisdom.

Some of the speakers had free downloads in exchange for my email which I proffered with enthusiasm. I saved all the information in a designated computer file and reviewed the offers. Among them was an invitation to join a free blogging boot-camp by *Elite Blogging Academy*[26] (EBA). Since I had learned that I needed to develop a platform from which to introduce my book, and that the best way to do this was by building an audience via a blog, this was another well-timed step toward my intentions.

I don't know what I expected but when the boot-camp began in the private Facebook group, it involved setting up a self hosted website! This involved money and decisions and I quickly became overwhelmed. For a few days I shut down completely just to contemplate how I was going to proceed.

A monetary investment needed to be made so Shawn and I sat down to discuss the cost and he set a reasonable amount for me to spend for the necessities only. I completed the tasks of setting up my website just as the boot-camp instructed but our budget did not allow for the enrolment into EBA's wonderful blogging course. This course promised to teach me how to blog to financial success. It looked and sounded wonderful but investing in it would take all the money we had set aside to invest

---

[26] Learn more and access free resources from Elite Blogging Academy:
https://eliteblogacademy.com/resources/

leaving nothing for the necessary, practical expenses of actually running the blog.

I wasn't the only person grieving this shortage of funds and feeling lost as to what to do next. Someone in that EBA blogging boot-camp had the wherewithal to suggest we start a separate private Facebook group where all of us capital-short funded aspiring bloggers could carry the torch of desire until the following year where we would hopefully have the savings to start EBA on the next round. Joining this group was the third strategic decision I made toward my goal.

In that group we were peppered with offers from other "Blogging How-To" courses. Some by blogging entrepreneurs who had stealthily joined the boot-camp and followed us into our new group and others by participants like myself who had stumbled upon a great resource. Our group became a wealth of resource suggestions and advice. A place where we could ask our newbie questions and someone would give us a link to the answers. I realize now that what we were doing was called "crowd sourcing". All I know is that it was exactly what I needed.

Somehow, I continued my journey in that fashion and that is how I ended up here writing to you without paying for a single course or class! Not that I wouldn't have loved to sign up for any number of those wonderful blogging courses, it just wasn't feasible if I wanted to stay on my unpaid sabbatical.

Having been immersed in this blogging/writing online community for four months now, I have become aware of something that I want to share with you. Maybe you know this already but if you don't, you need to.

There are entrepreneurs whose whole business model is built on showing you their "secrets" to successfully achieving your dream so buyer beware. I'm not saying that these businesses are bad and I don't want to paint them as fraudulent. It's just that there is a labyrinth of free information out there for the taking but there will also be a lot of successful, appealing opportunists in the mix that will try to convince you that without them and their service, you will fail. You will fail or you will miss the opportunity and waste valuable time "trying to figure it out on your own".

Why I bring this up is because at this critical juncture, I could have given up on my dream to blog and write a book. I don't have the money for that expensive course AND what they recommend so I'm done. My dream is done. I've failed before I've begun. If I had embraced the marketing jargon, I would have either spent money we didn't have which would send my sorry butt back to work or I would have frozen my dream indefinitely.

If it wasn't for my crowd-sourcing Facebook community and our collaborative wisdom, I wouldn't have known what to do next, and next, and after that. Not that I don't have anything more to learn but if and when I ever do have the resources to invest in training after the fact, I will have to do some research because I suspect I've already picked up much of the average beginner course information already for free.

So, my friend, if you have a dream, beware of those who are promising you that they can take you there if only you pay $ _____. Even if they line up lots of testimonials and display their success, remember that many of those successful entrepreneurs are raking in a lot of money just to show you how to do the same thing to others. That's fine if that's what you want to do but if it isn't, then do you really want to learn their ways?

I just want you to remain true to your dream and do it in a way that is authentic to you without getting sidelined by those who will tell you that you can't succeed without them. You can if you are diligent to search, ask and listen. I kept telling myself that I would act on the free advice until I had completed all of it and then I would consider paying for more. I haven't come to the end of utilizing what I've already been given and I've discovered that it isn't the attaining of advice that is difficult, it is the exercise of it.

There are no shortcuts to achieving a dream. No amount of money you lay on the table is going to get you past the actual work needed to get there.

Chapter Twenty-Seven

Trading for Trinkets

As I commiserated earlier, we readily sacrifice the true gems of life for trinkets. The majority of people in North America are not trying to take care of the four basic necessities: Housing and Utilities (power and water), Transportation, Food and Clothing (basic).

I enjoy the extras as much as the next person but we often forget that Internet, cable, streaming subscriptions, gym memberships, restaurant dining, electronics, salon visits, recreation vehicles, vacations, luxury vehicles, mansions, pools, jacuzzi tubs and even pets are not necessities. They are luxuries of abundance.

There is no condemnation for those who have the means to enjoy these pleasures. I only wish to send out a warning as one who has worked and strived to the point of soul-starvation to achieve a life filled with these extras. If you are sacrificing your mental/physical health and relationships to have it all... it isn't worth it.

You will discover eventually that possessions will not prevent you from getting old, being lonely, experiencing loss or pain or sustain your will to live. As sparkly as acquisitions appear along with the satisfaction when you have finally made them your own, you will only be left hungry for more. The next thing will take its place in your mind.

It's hard to ignore the alarming trend in suicides. Successful, wealthy, attractive individuals are suffering mental illness and despair. This is not the stereotypical shamed, down-on-their-luck society outlier we would envision to be at risk. Does this not serve to warn us that "having it all" might not be the pinnacle of joy that we envision?

How can you know if you are living in the compromised state of trading for trinkets? Ask yourself these questions:

- *Do I have someone I can share my days activities with who listens?*

- *Do I have the time and emotional energy to be that person for other people?*

- *How are my relationships with my family? Do we enjoy time together or dread it?*

- *Are the people I work with happy to see me every day and likewise?*

- *Do I enjoy what I do or do I feel like I am serving a prison sentence?*

- *Do I feel like I have viable life options or have I painted myself into a corner?*

- *Am I living in accordance with my values?*

- *Am I healthy and vibrant or am I falling apart from bad choices?*

- *Do I sleep well at night or am I disturbed by insomnia, stress dreams or other sleep disruptions?*

- *Do I feel like I have enough time to do the things I need to do?*

- *Do I feel joy?*

- *Do I laugh?*

- *Am I chronically frustrated and angry?*

If you don't like the answers to these questions you may be overdue for some rest, reflection and life change. It is likely that the suggestion sounds wonderful to you but if you are like the majority of people, it is unattainable. Why?

Rest, reflection, and life change demand that you let go of the extras, the luxuries that we simultaneously despise and long for. We despise them because they hold us trapped in our quest to attain them and yet we long to have them at any cost to ourselves and others.

Thus, the anger and frustration.

If you are like me you may be abusing something to cope with this dilemma. For me it was food and spending but for others it is alcohol, drugs, illicit sex, porn, smoking, and a host of other activities to help get the "edge off". I promise you this coping activity is only fuelling a vicious cycle of dependence because these vices only add to the list of pleasures. We must be willing to let go of them if we want to be free.

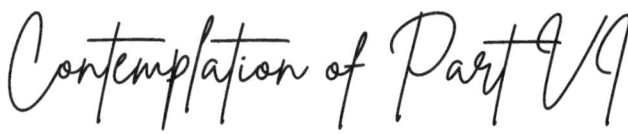
Contemplation of Part VI

1. Would your current financial situation allow you to slow down and rest as described in the previous section? If not, why?

2. Are you in debt? If so, have you considered a radical shift in your financial approach to change that situation?

3. Do you think that the solution to your problem is to earn more, spend less or both? Please explain.

4. What could you give up to allow for more rest in your life?

5. Do you have hope for your financial and working situation? If not, what do you think could change that?

6. When you think about your ultimate goals and desires for your life and all you are doing to attain that; do you feel that you are on the right track or do you think you need to readjust?

7. Can you identify with the story summary of the Mexican fisherman? Are you working and spending incessantly in a search for something you can't earn or buy? If so, what is it you want and why?

8. Can you see where you are choosing one thing and by doing so you are not choosing something else? Are you happy with your choices? Do you want to change them?

9. Do you practise money-saving techniques like Shawn and Melissa do? If so, what are they?

10. In what ways could you improve your spending and saving habits?

11. Do you have multiple "side hustles" in addition to your job where you try to increase your income?

12. Have you experienced the success and wealth promised in comparison to the effort you are expending? If not, have you considered letting it go?

13. Do you feel like you've divided yourself into too many little slivers? If so, what parts of life are falling through the cracks?

14. Is your side-hustle just an extension of your spending? A desire for material goods or health products? If so, could you bring yourself to let it go? If not, what value is it adding to your life?

15. Have you ever been promised something by a marketer and been disappointed when the product or service didn't live up to its claim? If so, how?

16. Are you marketing savvy in terms of being able to weigh claims, read unsponsored reviews, listen to the wisdom of others and say no even when you feel an emotional pull?

17. Are you capable of following your dreams by making the most of free or lower cost advice and taking action at whatever level you can or do you always feel that you are limited by your ability to invest?

18. At the end of the day, do you feel like you are trading your valuable resources for the life your truly want or do you feel like you are trading for trinkets. Please explain.

19. Do you feel like the things you own and have achieved have brought you the happiness and fulfilment you thought they would? If not, what would you trade them for?

Notes

Part VII: Economy of Happiness

Chapter Thirty

Rest Costs Less

hen I initially drafted an updated budget for my year off work, it felt almost apocalyptic. No salon haircuts or colourings, no nail salon visits, reduced grocery and entertainment amounts. We made cuts in many categories. I was terrified but determined.

We could live without "the extras" for one year, right? I was willing to sacrifice anything for that temporary reprieve.

At the time, we had roughly $10,000 on a line of credit that we were not paying down despite our monthly payments. We had become very lax in our healthy spending habits for the first time since our initial debt reduction. Every month, our expenses were exceeding our earnings just a little bit purely because we had very little incentive to pay attention to proper balance. My husband was concerned about me quitting work for a year with this debt looming over us.

I forged ahead with my resignation but it took a full three months to find and hire a replacement. In that time, we started to make most of the projected financial changes even though I was still working.

The crazy amazing thing was that in less than four months from that decision, we had paid off that line of credit. It was dizzying.

The emotional drive and energy I gained once I made the choice to take a break from work fuelled hope that gave me the necessary wherewithal to reduce spending and funnel every dime to our debt.

Seeing that single financial obstacle melt with the power of focus gave me confidence that we would not only survive a year of reduced income, we would thrive. I was sure of it.

At the time of this writing we are seven months into my sabbatical and still running our lifestyle debt-free.

How have we done this?

I have termed it "Economy of Happiness". When we exist in our authentic states, living in our passion and experiencing life as it is meant to be lived free from the mindset of perfection and performance, we don't need to spend nearly as much as when the opposite is true.

I had no idea how many little purchases I made purely out of maintaining an image, unhappiness or attempting to cope. I had no idea how much money I spent just for the privilege of working! Our auto fuel, clothing and haircare budget went down dramatically. At home I was comfortable in gym clothes and my previous work wardrobe was more than enough for the occasional times I needed to "dress up".

I purchased a pair of hair cutting scissors and a hair cutting tool then used a YouTube tutorial to learn how to cut my own hair. I bought store hair dye kits to touch up my grey roots.

My vehicle is parked most of the week which saves on fuel and our insurance reduced slightly because I became an occasional driver.

I wear makeup if I'm going out which is only a few times a week, so I save on cosmetics.

I have the time to do my own manicures, pedicures, facials and other upkeep.

We just kept finding pockets of spending that wasn't necessary because of our lifestyle change.

Occasionally, when I am tempted to spend beyond our means I ask myself, "Am I willing to trade the life I enjoy now to pay for this item?"

Hint: The answer is always no.

I have the freedom to give away the beautiful, restful pace I enjoy anytime. I just can't do it when I know how precious relaxed living is to me and my family. The price is way too high.

I would challenge any family to look at what they spend to maintain their employment to decide if trimming some luxuries might be worth the benefit reducing work hours to create margin in their schedules.

Chapter Twenty-Nine

Time Share

felt incredibly selfish taking a year off to take care of myself even though I know my mental and physical health made it a priority. My husband hedged at the idea of carrying the burden of our finances alone but I know he saw how desperate I was.

In addition to the economy of happiness we experienced in our finances, we also experienced a delightful shift in our home as I became rested and relaxed.

Initially, with the whole year spanning in front of me, I got extra motivated around the home. The house got a cleaning from top to bottom with furniture getting moved and spaces being organized.

I would get Shawn's tea ready before he got downstairs in the morning and I took on his household chores. As much as was possible, I wanted him to be free of duties that I could do myself. He has enough projects that I am incapable of performing.

I took a renewed interest in the bedroom.

I was cooking and food prepping more consistently.

The dogs were walked and bathed more regularly.

I was able to chauffeur my son when taking the bus wasn't optimal.

Shawn and I started exercising together.

It was a wonderful shift that affected the health and wellbeing of our entire household.

I will admit that once I discovered my passion for writing and developing my blog, I lost some of my attentiveness. It is so-far a non-paid venture that absorbs a lot of time and attention even if it brings me huge happiness and fulfilment.

Still, I am much more rested and available to my family than I once was and I constantly hope to strike that elusive balance in the home. It's not perfect but it's so much better than it was.

In addition to my challenge to look at your family's "economy of happiness", I suggest that you talk about what tasks and chores could be taken on by the person who is thinking about coming home. How would that shift relieve the burdens of those who continue to work? You may be surprised to find, as we did, that everyone benefits.

Chapter Thirty

Setting Down Agendas

I had a problem that is common to all who are particularly busy with managing their many responsibilities. My overflowing schedule was creating a near narcissistic lifestyle which made it difficult to have connecting relationships. It wasn't that I didn't care about others, want to help, or allow others to lead. It was that I felt like I was drowning in my own work. I was checking off my to-do list to hopefully get to that itty-bitty sliver of indiscriminate leisure time every day and nothing was going to knock me off track in getting there. Unless my plans or time with others was conducive to my own agenda, I was not remotely interested or even if I was, felt powerless to lay down my own agenda to be part of someone else's.

Without meaning to, you become the person who gathers friends and family around your plans and desires but opts out of being part of theirs because you are "too busy". Your life becomes incapable of any interruption or detour. Every red light, technology malfunction, miscommunication, and altered plan becomes a huge obstacle to your destination and you find yourself swatting down potential disruptions. You close your eyes to distraction and beauty around you because of your laser focus on your own goals. If certain people don't fit into your goals, then they become irrelevant — only to become relevant again if they show some value to furthering your own plans.

I could see my tendency to be that way and prayed often that God would help me change so I could genuinely love people better.

My journey toward being the kind of wife, mother, daughter, sister, and friend that I truly want to be improved vastly when I set down my work responsibilities for a season of rest. I'm a work in progress. I think my personality will always struggle with having huge goals and a tendency to be laser focused on them but by slowing down and adopting a lifestyle of creating margin in my time and finances, I will do much better. If you struggle with this issue, so will you.

One example of this happened just this weekend. My husband wanted to go for a motorcycle ride and couldn't find a friend to ride with him last minute. He poked his head into the laundry room where I was folding our clothes and asked me if I wanted to go with him. I hesitated for a moment as I thought about my eagerness to be finished with my tasks and this laundry folding was the last obstacle to me enjoying my own leisure activities on this day. Shawn doesn't usually ask me to join him because he knows I don't like or feel safe on his motorcycle so this was a rare request on his part. I decided to put aside my own leisure agenda and accept his.

It ended up being a very enjoyable time together. The weather was the perfect blend of warmth and cool breeze. We chatted through Bluetooth technology in our helmets and I pondered why I'm not typically open to sharing this activity with him more often. The truth is that I could pick up the personal leisure time I was sacrificing on the following day while he went to work. When I had been working full-time, that wouldn't have been an option. The personal discretion time following that laundry folding could have been my only opportunity in the entire week to do a hobby or project that meant something to me so my answer to his request would have been a definite no. He came to realize this and had stopped asking at all even though I'm sure at times he would've enjoyed my company.

That's only one example. There are probably many more friends and family who mentally think of asking me to partake in an activity that I've rejected in the past due to busyness or preference, who have simply stopped asking because my answer was always no.

I'm not a neighbourhood social butterfly either. I'm not good with names so I get embarrassed when I come across a neighbour that I've met numerous times over the years and still cannot recall their name. For years I had a hectic schedule that kept me from being the kind of person who hung around outside visiting with those on my street, I am slowly coming out of my shell as I walk my dogs everyday. It feels foreign but nice to stop and chat with neighbours along my route for a few minutes. For many this may seem trivial but for me it is a huge step.

Of course, there is a balance to this. In order to keep my life pace uncluttered and meaningful, I can't say yes to everything. This isn't a total setting down of my own purposes and carte blanche to join everyone else's. It's just a beautiful glimpse now and then that I have the flexibility and freedom to be generous with my time when I see opportunities to love and connect with others in a way that has previously eluded me due to workload.

Chapter Thirty-One

Minimalism

The more I journey toward rest, the more the concept of minimalism appeals to me. Sometimes it is not so much our cluttered schedules that are causing us distress so much as the clutter in our homes.

Having started my married life in a one-bedroom apartment, I noticed a whole lot of difference between the time it took to clean that space compared to our first house. Then when we bought the home we live in now; I saw another significant change.

I went from having one washroom to clean to four. We felt a little pinched in our apartment and I remember that our first house had empty rooms when we first moved in. Over a decade we filled that house with a couple extra little people and a whole lot of stuff. When we moved, we did the same thing. At first our new home felt spacious and then in a very short time, we claimed every inch of space and sometimes I feel overly full.

When we drive through ritzy neighbourhoods and I see the huge homes that I once coveted, now I can only think one thing: I would never want to have to clean that house! Isn't that funny? All I see is more square footage that I would need to take care of and I'm already overwhelmed with what I currently have.

I feel the same way when I see a large property or a pool. More work. More money. More mowing and filtering. We have a fairly small back yard and we barely use it at all. Why would I want more? I make time to visit our community pool one or two times a week. Why would I want to take care of one? It's different if you can afford to hire help and some people genuinely enjoy these tasks but it's not our preference. No thank you! We are open to enjoying other people's yards and pools occasionally. Smile.

I like my gidgets and gadgets in the kitchen but overall, I've been told by some that my house is a little sterile. We don't have a lot of places to display knick knacks and I hate both dusting and dusty stuff so collectibles for display has never been a thing for me.

Kitchen appliances, craft supplies, and gym equipment is another matter. I like working out and making stuff, edible and otherwise. I also like to organize it in bins, boxes and on shelves for easy access.

Cleaning, organizing, rearranging, sorting, maintaining...these are the time-consuming and sometimes expensive by-products of owning a lot of stuff. We don't realize it because we've just become accustomed to it.

I read some of the Jack Reacher series by Lee Childs. If you aren't acquainted with Jack Reacher's persona, it is extremely minimalistic, far beyond most minimalists. His character is a former military drifter who carries a fold-able toothbrush, some money, a passport and a debit card. He buys clothing that he wears and rinses out until it is too soiled to continue wearing -- typically within three days. He then buys a whole new outfit and repeats the process.

When questioned about his habits, he reasons that more possessions only serve to needing more and more until he would have to have a house to store them in. If he had the house then he would have the mortgage and then also the job. More leads to more.

It's extremely intriguing even if you don't agree or even wish for that kind of freedom. The truth is that our white picket fence dreams necessitate a lot of stuff that ends up weighing us down in life.

I'm no Jack Reacher. I like my home and its belongings but there's a constant valuing and revaluing of our home contents. How much time am I spending in all the activities of accumulating and caring for them? What can we get rid of and what gives value to our lives? How much are we spending to organize and store our stuff?

When I look around and realize we have too much and we're spending too much time arranging and rearranging it, I feel stress. That is why I'd rather lean toward minimalism when and where I can and it's getting easier to let go as the years go by.

If you have clutter, I definitely recommend a good cleaning out. Watch some YouTube videos on minimalism and get some ideas. Go through your stuff and pare it way back.

One concept that helps me a lot is to see my life and home like a stream. A vibrant, fresh-water stream has flow, water feeding in and draining out. By comparison, a marsh or swamp has water that flows in but doesn't drain out. The result is cloudy, stagnant water that doesn't flow. It's not drinkable or nice for swimming either.

A person who buys and fills their home with belongings but never allows belongings to leave, is a hoarder and their home resembles a swamp. A person who buys, even if in excess at times, but gives, sells or throws away a ratio of belongings by comparison is a life-giving stream.

That's why it is a good practise to let go of possessions when you bring new belongings home. That's also why it is a good practise to minimize what you bring home in the first place.

Contemplation of Part VIII

1. What did you think about some of the sacrifices Melissa made to enjoy a sabbatical year? Could you see yourself doing the same thing?

2. What expenses are you paying for the privilege of working? (Childcare, clothing, jewellery, travel expenses etc.)

3. In what ways could you economize if you had more time?

4. What behaviours do you use to cope with your busy lifestyle and how could you possibly reduce those if you were to slow down?

5. In what ways could you increase your family's ability to rest if you were less encumbered with work obligations yourself?

6. Do you ever find yourself so buried in your own schedule's demands that you find it impossible to fit into other people's plans for any length of time? If so, explain.

7. How do you think that being less busy would affect your relationships with others?

8. Is it possible that you are hiding behind your work to avoid relationships? If so, how and why?

9. Do you think you could be more relational without being overly drawn into plans that would upset your balance of work and rest? What would your boundaries be?

10. What do you think about the concept of minimalism?

11. Are you stressed out by excess clutter or possessions that require excessive upkeep? If so, do you have a plan to adjust that?

12. Do you see your home as a swamp or a stream? What small things could you do to improve?

13. Are you adept at determining if an item will really "spark joy" long term BEFORE you buy it? If not, what can you do to change that?

14. Knowing that most seniors have to offload most of their possessions as their strength and ability to care for them lessens, how does that impact your buying choices now?

15. How much lighter would your life be if you didn't have to spend hours cleaning and organizing so much stuff?

Notes

Part VIII: Slowing Down Your Mind

Chapter Thirty-Two

Slow Down is the New Miracle Cure

The rush starts before I even open my eyes in the morning. Thoughts of what needs to be done literally rouse me from sleep. Then there's the notifications on the phone as my eyes adjust to the screen glare. Emails. Calendar. Sleep readings. Bible App. Facebook. Maybe not in that order either. Before I've had my morning coffee, I've gone through dozens of digital tasks and my mind is buzzing.

Then, coffee in hand, I'm ready for action. Feed the dogs, prepare breakfast and other food needed for the day, all while listening to funny comedy clips or videos from my favourite subscribes. I'd hoped to sit down to read and reflect before officially starting my day but that window has passed and now, I'm just hoping that I hit all the deadlines for the day.

Sounds like I might be a busy, working mom, right? Well that would be a no. I quit my job months ago. My kids are grown up and only one lives at home. I literally have full control of my schedule for the first time in my adult life.

So why is life still going full speed? The only answer I have is that the busyness is a behaviour I've learned and it has become a habit.

I've managed to limit the external demands on my time but the internal push is unrelenting. I sometimes catch myself holding my breath and mentally panicking about everything on my to-do list, a to-do list that I put together. I realized that my own expectations and habits were cluttering my mind and pushing me onward.

Deep breath. It's going to be okay. I'm going to do as much of that list as I can and then I'm going to pick up where I left off tomorrow.

Another deep breath. When did I become like this? I try to remember when I didn't live my days with low grade anxiety about everything that had to be done and by when. I can't. Well, maybe it started in earnest when I became a mother over 20 years ago. That's when I started drinking coffee...

Now I realize that a lifetime of stress tasking isn't just going to magically stop the moment I give myself permission to relax. The adrenaline that propelled me through years of diapers, potty training, bus stop pickups, appointments, jobs, renovations, volunteer shifts and classes...is still coursing through my veins.

The ironic thing is that even with a wide-open schedule I still feel like I am failing. I'm still not meeting up to the demands of my "list".

It made me realize that slowing down is an internal state of mind. It is a harnessing of the mind and emotions that needs to happen in little deliberate bits every single day of my life...not in some far off "when I've achieved everything on my list" life mirage. That day never comes.

Chapter Thirty-Three

The Altar of Efficiency

My friend and I walk together and we agreed that we both justify the time because it meets two needs: exercise and social interaction.

Multitasking.

As a child growing up, I remember listening to motivational teachings and reading books that glorified the skill of doing more than one thing at once. The better you were at doing everything at once, the more successful you would be.

It was a waste of valuable time to do only one thing at a time. You must be killing two birds with one stone and juggling a mayhem of people and activities to be a productive person.

I bought into this completely and in all honesty still do it. It's not wrong to multitask so you can accomplish things efficiently, it's just that there is a time to put that aside and slow everything down as much as possible.

Have you ever been multi-tasked? Maybe met with someone who you knew was juggling you along with everything else they had to do? How did that make you feel? Lousy, right?

Some things won't work in efficiency mode.

You might think you've made it just to check mark something off your list but I guarantee you, something was lost.

As a married couple with children, including a special needs son, working, volunteering and renovating our home...we multi-tasked a lot. We had a divide and conquer survival mode going full force. You watch this one and I'll watch that one. I'll fix the house and you go buy the groceries. Normal stuff that couples do to cut through all the demands and hopefully find some time together at the end.

Only sometimes that just made me feel terribly alone and disconnected except for brief times on the weekend.

Over time, I got better at communicating to my husband when it was necessary to throw efficiency out the window to do things together. It was really hard for my husband and I was torn about putting my emotional needs out there because it affected me too. Only I had to because the pain of living a life driven by efficiency was too much.

It made me realize that just like someone can be good with their finances to the point of being a miser, a person can also be so good with their time that they become stingy there too.

Since I refer to the Bible as a standard for my priorities and values, I wondered that I never saw the word "multitask" or "efficiency" in the text even once. Oh yes, there are admonishments to be wise, to utilize time well and not be lazy but there's no commandments about needing to do multiple things at once and race through life juggling tasks to the point of dropping everything.

That's when I realized that just as someone can make an idol of money, a person can also worship at the altar of efficiency. While some sins are easy to spot and condemn, others appear virtuous but they erode at our ability to connect with each other and even with God.

My husband and I have been guilty of this. We are recovering but it's taking time to shift our performance and perfectionist mindsets to remember that people and joy are more important than accomplishment.

Every once in a while, I allow my day to be rearranged out of the order that I would have planned so I remember that efficient isn't always better. I'm still a work in progress when it comes to finding that elusive balance.

Another type of multitasking is mind distraction. I like to play movies or YouTube videos while I work in the kitchen or fold the laundry. Sometimes though, I purpose to do the work quietly instead and tune in to my thoughts. Be fully present. If I am playing any media, I purpose to turn it off when a loved one comes into the room. Even if they aren't talking to me, just to provide the opportunity for acknowledgement and conversation if needed.

Our work, entertainment and to-do lists will always be there but it's vital to realize that you can be the richest, most productive person in the world and be the most lonely, unfulfilled at the same time. Better to have less money and accomplishments and share life with others who love you.

If you struggle with too much multi-tasking and efficiency-overdrive I advise that you start setting that aside especially when dealing with people. Turn off the phone, try to give your full attention, add a little margin in your calendar, and keep life simple.

Contemplation of Part VIII

1. Do you ever find yourself experiencing low-grade anxiety or feeling rushed for no reason at all? If so, when and why?

2. Do you have the ability to slow down after an extended period of time at a frantic pace? If so, how do you transition?

3. Do you ever have to get to the end of your to-do list so you feel you have permission to relax or do you work until you're so exhausted that you're incapable of doing a meaningful relaxation activity?

4. How does practising a regular rhythm of work and rest better prepare you for "turning off" the stress later in life?

5. Do you find it difficult to do one task at a time? If so, which activities do you pair together?

6. Multitasking in itself isn't wrong but are there times where you know that it would be better to give your full attention to one task? If so, which ones specifically?

7. How do you cope when the power goes out and your electronics are unavailable for use for a few hours?

8. Do you ever find yourself denying yourself opportunities for love and connection in the pursuit of efficiency? If so, when and why?

9. Do you struggle with being present with the people in your life while tasks are left undone? If so, what do you think is driving that struggle?

10. Have you ever wanted to spend time with someone and you know you don't have their full attention? How does that feel? Have you done that to others?

11. What can you do to slow down and be present for meaningful connection more often?

Notes

Part IX: A Matter of Health

Chapter Thirty-Four

KonMari Your Heart

S ometimes our need for rest can stem from a build up of emotional garbage. Hurt feelings, offences, disappointments... The load of unresolved emotions grows and ferments in our hearts. Sometimes our need for rest is from warring against people and situations that constantly press against or even violate our boundaries again and again.

Whatever the situation or reason, if you are feeling negative emotions that are thrusting you toward a season of rest, it is imperative to address that.

For me, I was facing ongoing work and ministry politics that I found draining, some disappointment in family life and a sense of having hit a ceiling in a ministry career that I was pretty sure I didn't even want. When I resigned, I found the reactions to my decision to be a mix of congratulations, scepticism and outright awkward silence with unvoiced disapproval.

Another thing that stirred up agitation for me was that at the time there were major celebrations of other's transitions "up the ministry ladder" but my decision to step back felt uncelebrated. What I was undertaking felt extremely spiritual to me but since it didn't look or sound prestigious, it felt swept under the carpet. I got the sense that my actions were interpreted as falling short of a bigger, better plan.

Of course, I saw my willingness to let go of everything to slow down my life as incredibly brave, necessary and a move toward spiritual maturity. I chalked up the lack of admiration and fanfare as part of the sacrifice. Being willing to be judged and misunderstood was part of the package. I'm not going to lie, it hurt a lot. I cried as I let go of my reputation and pride to follow what I knew in my heart was the right path for me.

There were other hurtful words and events that transpired as I transitioned out of my role and the result was that when I finally landed at home, I was feeling traumatized and confused about a lot of my relationships. What had happened? How could the simple decision to leave my job and the effort to do so responsibly have gone so terribly wrong?

At the same time as this was unfolding, Marie Kondo's book, "The Life-Changing Magic of Tidying Up: The Japanese Art of Decluttering and Organizing[27]", was sweeping North America. I had recently completed a road trip where my girlfriend streamed Marie's audio-book for a good part of our 15-hour drive. When I emerged from the vehicle, I had mysterious symptoms that I later discovered were the onset of sciatica.

A month later with my job transition wrapped up, I remember being physically and emotionally devastated having gone into full-on sciatic flare-up to the point of just lying on my couch for a few weeks crying and in pain trying to process not

---

[27] Learn more about The Life-Changing Magic of Tidying Up: The Japanese Art of Decluttering and Organizing https://amzn.to/2TU4k5z

only my physical symptoms but my emotional ones as well. I decided to give the first 30 days of my sabbatical to the process of forgiveness so that I could clear out all this emotional junk and move on with my year unencumbered.

There are many great books and sermons on forgiveness as it is a core foundation to the Christian faith I grew up in. However, in my case, it wasn't until I read a book called, "*The Freedom Factor: Finding Peace by Forgiving Others*[28]", by Bruce Wilkinson, that I found a practical guide that made sense to me. In his gentle, but tough-love book, I found some principles that helped me realize that there was likely a correlation between the emotional angst I was experiencing and my physical symptoms. Bruce provides a practical step-by-step forgiveness exercise that gave me a tangible way to process relational hurts in a manner that helped truly diffuse and heal wounds that kept resurfacing. It's a series of practical steps that help you pick the burrs of anger, hurt and offence out of one's heart one by one.

---

[28] Learn more about The Freedom Factor: Finding Peace by Forgiving Others: https://amzn.to/2KQkud4

I decided that it was worthwhile to delay my other plans and focus on active forgiveness first. I read Bruce's book and started practising his forgiveness exercises, starting with the most painful issues first. It's not hard, just time consuming and emotionally taxing. The results were amazing though. I started to heal and day by day found the strength to get back to my original purpose for taking the break.

The following month, Marie Kondo's Netflix series aired and, still limited by sciatic symptoms, I watched all the episodes while knitting. It was very interesting to watch people's lives blossom when they freed themselves of the junk they were hoarding.

The physical purging I was witnessing in the Netflix episodes matched the spiritual purging I was practising in my forgiveness journey so much, that I coined the phrase, "KonMari Your Heart". I developed my own forgiveness process to share with readers on my blog. It's a simple 4-day email coaching series that uses elements from Marie Kondo's tidying up system as a model for releasing forgiveness.

I can't emphasize the value of forgiveness and correct processing of emotions enough because it allows us to heal and the replenished emotional energy helps us to take care of ourselves in other ways too.

After dealing with my emotional pain I found the strength to clean my home, then complete gentle exercises and continued to make healthful decisions. Now months later I am free from all symptoms of sciatica. In fact, I am thriving in every area!

Chapter Thirty-Five

Recognizing the Problem

I mentioned several times that my health was not in the best place when I started my sabbatical year. That is an understatement. It was at its worst.

A lifelong struggle with food was coming to a climax and my battle with living a mostly sedentary existence was killing my metabolism. My muscles and joints were not strong to the point that I was hurting myself doing simple, basic activities: driving, sleeping, turning. For a person who has placed a lot of value on health and fitness for most of my life, this was embarrassing!

Like most people, I blamed my situation on long, sedentary work hours, a busy schedule, out of control life and lack of motivation due to feeling trapped. I was positive that as soon as I was free from my busy work schedule, I would immediately bounce back to my previous healthy existence. No one was more shocked than I was when that didn't happen.

As I mentioned in the previous chapter, I had onset symptoms of sciatica after a long road-trip and didn't fully realize it until the first few days at home after leaving my job. What I didn't mention is that it was my initial attempt to resume regular workouts that caused the underlying injury to flare-up fully. The pain from my left hip to toe was more extreme than I'd ever experienced before. It was difficult to sit never mind move. I realized right then that I had to heal before I could get fit. I was "a fragile egg". This is a term that my past fitness instructor training used to define fitness participants who can "break" easily if introduced to fitness too intensely at first. Fortunately, my previous experience as a personal trainer and fitness instructor gave me the knowledge and wisdom I needed to treat myself as such.

I went for therapy appointments and my first workouts were in our local pool. I like to swim but I always treated it like a supplementary exercise to more vigorous routines. Now it was literally all I was capable of other than daily walks with my dogs. More than that, I had huge post workout soreness from those two mild activities! I hurt and ached!

Fortunately, I didn't give up. I couldn't. If I wanted to recover, the only way to do so was to keep going.

Then after a month, Shawn asked if I could start trying to clean the house. I'd been blessed with cleaning help every couple weeks while I worked but that luxury was gone due to my lack of income. I wanted to clean my own home. To lay my hands on everything and organize as I went. I found the experience very satisfying and grounding. I also found it exhausting in a way I never before experienced.

I realized that brief workouts were one step forward but I was adjusting a body that was used to sitting 8-12 hours a day to standing for 6-8, along with the pushing and pulling, lifting and bending motions that cleaning requires. Again, I was embarrassed at my lack of strength and stamina. I would tap out at around 3-4 hours and then literally could not move the next day. How did I get like this?

The therapy, light exercise, and consistent household activity was enough to see me out of the sciatica. I was so relieved that my body had healed! The likelihood of a repeat flare-up is high so I am determined to continue with my fitness journey judiciously to insulate myself from that risk.

Five months into my sabbatical my husband and I evaluated our ideal fitness habits compared to what we were doing. We instituted three exercise sessions a week to do weight training together. This was the first time we had aligned our schedules to a realistic expectation and actually stuck to it the majority of time. We look forward to those exercise sessions and make them enjoyable by watching a light-content program on Netflix and chatting while we do our separate routines. Sometimes we just "put in time" while the other works out but we show up and do something. We don't try to control the other persons workout or effort in any way except to boot each other off equipment now and then. This newfound harmony in our workouts was an exciting benefit of my flexible schedule.

I thought with my increased activity and new stress-free lifestyle that my eating would fall into place and I'd start to lose weight naturally. Boy, was I ever in for a shock when the opposite happened. My eating became more compulsive. I was hungry all the time and snacking to satisfy it. I was trying to follow a popular food plan but no matter how much I used my available time to plan, shop and cook, I could not stay in the daily food intake limits.

I found myself running to the refrigerator every couple hours. I just could not stop thinking about food and eating. My first episodes of eating to the point of acid reflux began within a month of starting my sabbatical. This was a new symptom for me. Before this year the only time I experienced acid reflux was during my pregnancies.

I wondered if my extreme fasting prior to my sabbatical had slowed my metabolism and was causing the compulsive eating in response. I continued trying to follow the popular food plan and watched my weight climb consistently as I failed.

My health suffered yet another blow when I started having mysterious back pains that reminded me of back labour. It got so severe that I went to the clinic and was diagnosed with my very first bladder infection. I was prescribed my first antibiotics in over 20 YEARS!

This diagnosis confused me because I'd heard other women explain the symptoms they experienced during their bladder infections and I didn't have those. I just had this persistent back pain that would creep around my rib cage and take my breath away. I went for blood tests and an ultrasound. Nothing. Fortunately, the back pain disappeared as soon as my antibiotic prescription was finished and didn't return. I still have no idea what was going on but I realized that this infection, whatever it was, was just another indication that my body was inflamed and something needed to change.

I decided to try another dietary approach that minimized carbohydrates and found that my body responded better to this than the other plan. I purposed to avoid unhealthy mistakes I had made in executing a low carbohydrate plan in the past. I lost a few pounds initially and was thrilled but then my weight just stuck. By all accounts I was doing everything right and testing showed that I was successfully eliminating excess carbohydrates. I was staying closer to my daily macro goals using this plan then with the other plan. I chalked this up again to a damaged metabolism and reasoned that if I felt good, was not gaining, and was eating in a stabilized way, then good enough was good enough.

Little did I know that this change in eating strategy was setting the stage for a deeper change that was necessary if I wanted to break free from my continued lifetime battle with food. A friend invited me to be her accountability buddy and we met over coffee to determine how we could support each other. As part of her plan she was going to go to a private accountability group that met every week at a local church. I offered to go with her to check it out.

When I entered the building, I was expecting a lecture style meeting with a leader at the front and the group passively listening. If I was bored, I could browse my phone to pass the time. Instead, I entered a classroom where a small group of women circled a table and the meeting required everyone to pay attention, make eye contact, respond to sharers and to share oneself.

I panicked right away. I recognized a couple people in the group in addition to my friend. The group structure resembled a tight, rule-based society that I was unaccustomed to and I felt an odd desire to get away and never return. Reminding myself that I was a grown-up and no-one was forcing me to stay, I decided to give the group a fair chance. By the end I was feeling more comfortable and when I read their materials and contemplated their mission, I had to admit that this group was probably an answer to prayer.

Maybe finally I would confront the issues that caused me to overeat and extreme diet in the first place. Maybe fitness could be less about burning calories so I could eat more food and more about what it needed to be: keeping myself healthy.

Chapter Thirty-Six

Confronting the Lies

I n my very first meeting we read some materials and listened to some sharing that really struck my heart. I realized that like me, a lot of the women sitting around the table were actually very disciplined in their eating the majority of the time. The issue was that their disordered relationship with food would inevitably cause them (and me) to overeat.

Even though I knew something was wrong with me in the area of food and dieting, I just couldn't put a finger on it. I kept throwing my best willpower at it.

Here in this weekly meeting time, with these precious women who were as broken as I was, I was finally ready to start identifying and confronting the lies I had been telling myself for years and to be free.

At the time of this writing I have just started this journey but because it isn't about the change of macros but rather of a focus on how I think and behave around consuming those macros...I know that this is a unique, life-changing journey.

As an example of some of the "revelations" I experienced this first week alone, I will share some of the changes I'm making based solely on what I've learned so far.

1. Despite my life-long Christian faith and my constant prayers to God regarding my weight and struggle with food, I often neglect to truly pray before I eat. Instead, we use mealtime prayer more when we are gathered as a family. As part of my recovery I recognize this to be a disordered approach to food in light of my core beliefs. I'm committed to praying a sincere prayer before diving into my food. This will be a sign of abstinence from overeating for me.

2. Diving into my food is a disorder for me. Anytime I slow down my eating pace, I eat less and digest better. This isn't new for me but I haven't paid it enough attention. Now that I'm aging and overeating (combined with poorly chewing my food), this

is causing digestive upset and weight gain in new ways, so this habit has to be addressed seriously.

3. Short term dieting is not good but choosing a reasonable life time eating plan is recommended so that you can have a healthy and realistic way to measure what eating is normal and what is excess. I had already picked an eating approach that was conducive to me and even though I was sticking "almost" to the daily macro limits, almost wasn't cutting it. I needed to confront the mindset in me that those daily limits were negotiable. I had to decide that abstinence, for me, was to stop eating when I had consumed all my daily macros. Period. That is a difficult one but important.

4. Stop manipulating the food plans. Every food plan has rules that can be manipulated to get the most pleasurable food possible. Even though most reasonable food plans include all foods, there are healthy foods that get eliminated or forgotten purely because there is no room for them in getting the most "bang for your food buck". In some plans, avocado or olives are pushed aside in order to have something else. In my

current meal plan, even small portions of fruit are neglected to make room for other carbohydrates. I determined to segment a certain number of my daily carbohydrates for fruit and have them at my first meal of the day so I wouldn't "forget" to eat them.

5. Long term diet means long term. In the past I found my dieting to be very isolating and so I would inevitably tire of being alone and disciplined. I would throw up my hands and tell my husband that he could choose our restaurants and I would make yummy treats for parties with my friends. Joining in with abandon would temporarily make me feel fun and connected but over the years the consequences of that have grown worse. I realize that I have to find connection in new ways. Isolation is the enemy. Healthy connection is my cure.

6. More exercise is not better. I used to exercise as much as I could so I could eat as much as possible. When I couldn't devote the time to exercise, I found it difficult to adjust my eating. Instead of using exercise for food consumption, my new priority is to use it in moderation for health and longevity

only; exercising for connection, pleasure and reflection. Like my food consumption, this needs to be consistent and maintainable, avoiding huge highs and lows that would contribute dramatic food intake fluctuations or energy crashes. Abusing exercise is just as damaging as abusing food.

7. I'm going to remain *the broken and not the fixer*. I have succeeded at many food plans in my life and with each success find people coming to me for guidance which inevitably contributes to my own decline. I can see that I could easily become proficient at this particular group style and be put in a position of leading. Unless some really big breakthroughs happen, I think that the dynamic of me trying to lead others to success in this area is something that needs to change. I see the repetition of this group mindset as being something that I will inevitably tire of and chafe under and yet submitting to it is likely the answer to my lifelong challenges. So long as I stop viewing myself as "the expert" and remain teachable, I will be able to receive the help I need.

I have no idea how the future is going to play out but I included this self-reflection here in this book because so many women I know are not only busy but extremely disordered in their relationship with food.

You may have a similar thought process that tells you if you could only get control of your life and slow down, then you would *automatically* eat and exercise properly. Then you wouldn't have the struggle you currently have.

I want to emphasize that this is false. It won't happen automatically. You can take the busyness out of your environment but unless you take the time and connect with the people that will help you confront your interior life; you will still suffer chaos within.

Take time to rest, do the healthy things and confront the lies that keep you unhealthy and sabotaged over and over again. Be patient with your "fragile egg" self and explore your brokenness. You can do this.

Chapter Thirty-Seven

Health Influencer

Just as the setting down of work on my behalf lead to a more restful existence for my entire household, so the addressing of my health and eating habits influenced every one in my home as well. I have noticed over the years that my family's nutrition always sat a few levels below my own. When I ate exceptionally well, their eating improved. When I threw up my hands and caved to indulgence, their nutrition would sink to deeper depths.

Naturally, when my emotional and physical health plummeted, the impact was felt by us all. Up until recently I was the only one who battled weight issues. However, in the past couple years I was noticing my husband and son were putting on the pounds in their midsections. Both my husband and I were warned by the doctor to lower our cholesterol.

The exciting thing about me investing in my personal well-being is that it has influenced my family positively. My husband has come along beside me and made remarkable progress not only in his ability to follow our new eating plan but in his commitment to invest in himself by taking daily time to workout. Naturally, his weight is dropping and I'm confident that his next blood test will show the desired results.

While we are not actively trying to recruit our son into our exercise and eating routine, I notice that he is taking cues from our newfound unity and making better choices than he made before. All this because mommy is getting her act together.

The wondrous thing about belonging to a family and being proactive in home life is that one person's performance or lack thereof impacts everyone else in that home. Even if our children aren't on board and don't look interested, they are watching everything we do very carefully.

This year has driven home the fact that I have so much more to offer my family than earning potential.

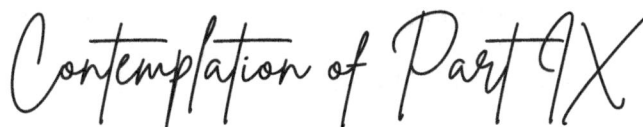
Contemplation of Part IX

1. Have you found yourself in a crisis where you found it necessary to practise forgiveness in order for you to get better and move on? If so, please explain.

2. Do you have a structured forgiveness process that you can use to deal with offences as they occur? If so, please explain.

3. Do you find that certain offences seem resolved but they reignite occasionally? If so, please explain.

4. Do you have people or situations you should forgive to make room for future growth and opportunities?

5. Have you ever had a problem that you thought would be fixed if you could only change your circumstances only to find out that the problem is inside you?

6. Is there a part of your life where you are a "fragile egg", a person who can be easily broken if given too much, too fast? If so, please explain.

7. Are you dealing with damage caused by past decisions that you thought were good only to find out they weren't? If so, please explain.

8. Is there an area of your life where you've made positive changes but the results don't show it yet? If so, please explain.

9. They say the opposite of addiction is not abstinence but connection. Are you working to build connections in your life to avoid isolation? If so, please explain.

10. Do you consider yourself a very disciplined person most of the time but find that the chaos during lapses of discipline sabotages your progress? If so, please explain.

11. Do you have noticeable gaps between what you believe and what you practise? If so, please explain.

12. Do you ever find yourself dismissing certain rules as not applying to you? If so, please explain.

13. Do you find yourself doing even good things to excess? Some is good, more is better? If so, please explain.

14. Do you recognize your realm of influence that is affected by your choices, either positive or negative? If so, please explain.

Notes

Part X: Braving Alone

Chapter Thirty-Eight

Alone

I t is important to realize that when you start to make changes in your life that others view as radically different than their own, you will hear their opinions both good and bad. If they are polite, they may say nothing and, in their confusion, pull back a little to watch what you are doing unfold.

It's also natural that as you step out of your role, the social dynamics around you will change.

I experienced this in the first few months of my sabbatical. Some of my text messages went unacknowledged, my initiations to get together for walks and talks with certain friends were rebuffed, and with some friends there was only conversation if I picked up the phone.

It's naive to think that you can turn your life upside down and not have ripple effects in your relationships. Just because you clear your schedule to make room for meaningful relationships doesn't mean other people will do the same thing.

I have to purposely remember what it felt like to be drowning in family, ministry, work and personal commitments. How did I feel to have a friend who wanted to spend time with me and as much as I wanted to, I would have to put off a visit because there just wasn't enough of me to go around? If the person made any comments about feeling neglected, I remember the flash of anger I would feel.

"Must be nice to have so much free time" was my mental jab toward someone who had more time than I did paired with a mix of jealousy, sadness and frustration that I was carrying such a heavy load.

I refuse to be that person. I won't apologize for setting down my load for a season of rest while my friends, family and acquaintances struggle with theirs but I won't try to make them feel guilty or add to their burden with condemning words either.

Once I mentally reflect on all this, I can depersonalize the feeling of being ignored or rebuffed and see it for what it really is. I want my time with friends to be a place where they feel refreshed and loved, not a place where they feel they need to apologize yet again for not being good enough.

This has worked well. Now I have enough coffee and exercise dates to fill my schedule to the point that I welcome the occasional lapse of social interaction.

Chapter Thirty-Nine

Saying No

Beyond the natural relationship shifting there is another challenge when you decide to give voice to the person inside you who isn't happy with the choices you made in the past by choosing differently. Not everyone will be happy with that decision. Be prepared to say no. A lot.

You would think that declaring that you need a rest and stepping back from your job for a year, a month or a week would give the necessary signal to the people around you that you are serious, but it is not. Busy people can literally smell someone who has time on their hands and they are often desperate to shift something, anything on to you.

At first this really angered me. Can't they see I'm trying to take a break? Do they think this is a game? Do they think I quit my paying job so I could take on their responsibilities? I honestly don't know what people are thinking but I got really adept at saying no.

It's not like I don't want to help people. It's just that it's okay to say no for a period of time. We're not talking about denial of *survival* help here. We're talking about things that people are perfectly capable of doing for themselves, finding or paying someone else or projects that can simply wait.

Are you a person who gets given a project by a friend or relative and once they assign it to you, they walk away to enjoy life with others? That happens to me sometimes and that's how I differentiate my "helping" during this rest season.

If someone wants to pay me to do something or hand off a responsibility, the answer is no. If they want to spend time with me...even if it involves a bit of something revolving around a project they are working on, I will likely say yes.

You want me to plan an event or do a job for you? No.

You want me to come over for a visit, and while we visit, discuss how to organize _____? Sure.

You want a visit and a drive to a medical appointment? Let's look at our calendar.

What I'm avoiding is huge time and energy commitments with very little relational reward. Period.

I'm refusing to lose even a moment of my sabbatical to anyone who would view me as a resource or worker to get their agenda done.

This is a lot harder than I thought it would be because I've considered myself pretty comfortable with saying no before. It's just usually it was because I was very busy with my own responsibilities. Saying no when your schedule is wide open and you are enjoying rest is completely different.

I've disappointed people. I'm going to disappoint people. It terrifies me. What if everyone I love turns their back on me like an unofficial shunning when they realize that I can no longer fit in the role they have cast for me?

I don't want people to think I'm selfish, uncaring or lazy. Some days I wrestle with this very tangibly but I really contemplate whether the person asking me to do something is in serious need or whether what they are asking is something I am morally compelled to do. In every case, it was not one of those two things.

When I feel the struggle to give in despite my resolve I think about my relationship with the person and what my motive would be to try to please them by saying yes. Am I being driven by a need to prove or perform? Am I trying to get their approval? Am I hoping that helping them will increase my relational equity with this person? Motivation is so important.

I woke up with these words in my head:

Sometimes the pain of giving what we can't afford

is what we endure to avoid being alone, but one day

we will have nothing left to give and we will have to

face that we were alone the whole time.

It's true. For years I did what was expected of me. I wrestled. I voiced dissent. Yet at the end of the day I gave into pressure and influence that told me what I wanted was selfish and wrong and what they wanted was right and good. I gave in because I knew that if I didn't there were hundreds of people who would take my place and I would be left behind. I never got what I truly wanted and now, years later, I'm facing the same dilemma. Conform to please others or be true to myself and be rejected. Not much of a choice, is it? I've tried conforming and now I must be brave and risk rejection.

Chapter Forty

Against the Tide

Have you ever felt yourself at odds with the crowd that you most identify with? You embrace the same mandate but you constantly find yourself questioning or differing in your expression. I have been on both sides of this equation: the person going against the tide and the one going with the tide trying to encourage someone to join in.

My experiences made me realize that there are different cultures even within a similar purpose or belief system. A person can find themselves at odds with the culture they find themselves in and still be very much in unity with the culture's higher purpose.

Having said that, after a time it may be wise to find a culture that resonates more with one's own expression as prolonged time living against the tide can build up frustration and loneliness.

I was once in charge of a fitness initiative experiment at my workplace and there was a co-worker who I know wanted to become fitter but they solidly refused to participate. I was initially puzzled by their refusal both because of their shared goal and because of their friendship with those who were participating, including my husband and me. It bothered me a little that they wouldn't participate. However, I soon realized that the group dynamic inside work hours conflicted with their preference to workout outside their employment, alone and reflective. Another co-worker who expressed desire to get fit also refused to participate because they valued their brief lunch period and used it to leave the premises every day. There were enough of these situations that I soon felt unappreciated in my efforts to bring fitness, stress relieving and team building opportunities so the experiment ended.

On the other hand, I found myself declining participation in a large annual women's conference that occurred every summer because although it perpetuated a common belief system and purpose, I found myself balking. There were elements of the event that just didn't work for me and on the few times I caved to pressures to participate, I left feeling regretful and disconnected. It took me a long time to come to terms with how my personality and preferences went against the tide of what so many other people enjoyed. I know my lack of interest and enjoyment troubled those who genuinely loved the activity.

My takeaway from this is that these situations are a great opportunity for discussion and understanding. Many "crowd" events are driven by extroverts and have dynamics that don't work for introverts. There are many ways to approach a common purpose and it is okay to not connect with every mainstream way of doing things.

Being brave enough to listen to one's inner voice even when it goes against "the norm" is a difficult, but special quality.

It's okay to want less so you can be more. It's okay to not be ambitious for greatness before the multitudes in order to be great in your home.

Listen to the cry of your heart when it tells you something different than the roar of others around you. Even if the trend they're following looks right and good, it may well be that you are being chosen to blaze a different trend that isn't acknowledged yet.

Sit with your feelings of having disappointed others. Look at your motivations. What is the cost of putting aside your emotions to conform and what is the cost of finding a different way? How long have you been suffocating the voice inside you that says, "This doesn't work for me?" If it has been years and years, then maybe its time to remove the gag and listen.

Listen. Not out of anger, resentment and rebellion. Not to destroy or put down the path that has gone before, but listen and examine what could be the same path but a new way.

Chapter Forty-One

Who Made the Rules Anyway?

There are so many times when I get caught up in events and activities then I suddenly realize that I don't even know why I'm doing what I'm doing. Have you ever experienced that? Sometimes it's because other people drafted me into their plans but sometimes it's stuff I came up with that sounded good and then I realize I don't even like it. Just today I caught myself making note of a local event and setting plans in motion to attend it before I caught myself. I realized that I was preparing to go out of a sense of duty even though I preferred to spend my time in a different way. It may sound peculiar, but I had to take myself off autopilot and get myself sorted before I made a time commitment that I would regret.

Someone gets an idea to go away for a weekend. Everyone is doing it, so when you get there, you wonder what in the world you were thinking when you agreed.

You're sitting with your family trying to think of something fun to do. Someone throws out an idea and everyone gets partway into it only to find that no-one really likes the activity.

Sometimes it's an activity that has become a ritual that far outlasts the enthusiasm for it. It's just always been that way and so it must continue.

There's a sentiment that says many times we spend money don't have on things we can't afford to impress people we don't even like. Sound familiar?

During our debt reduction days, we got really adept at examining our plans and saying no to things that we didn't want to spend our time and money on.

I want to say we're completely immune to people pleasing but sometimes we get swept up just like everyone else.

If you ever, ever feel pressure to spend your time or money in a manner that you either do not enjoy or even out of good intentions to please someone else, don't do it. Even if love is driving you, make sure it is a gift you can afford to give without betraying yourself. If you are doing it in hopes of receiving recognition, love or reciprocation in return, don't do it my friend. It's not worth it.

Sometimes we have negotiations where we have to give a little to make someone else happy and they do the same, that is fine but make sure it is a fair negotiation, not a folding of your cards.

I say this because it's important to remember that we are not victims and we have no one but ourselves to blame if we constantly give in to the requests or demands of others. We are obligated to say no and say it firmly if that is what is in our hearts. Anything less breeds resentment and is often just an avoidance of conflict.

This may be a good time to have some important conversations with your loved ones and friends. If you are enduring activities you don't like for business networking, you may want to rethink that business.

Life is give and take. No-one gets away with doing only the activities they love. However, if you are constantly giving and waiving your will to the point that you are heading away from a healthy life direction because of it, you need to review your situation.

Contemplation of Part X

1. Have you ever made a personal decision that left you open to misunderstanding and rejection? If so, please explain.

2. Have you ever made a decision that forced you to face being alone? If so, please explain.

3. Have you ever made a decision that caused an awkward shift in how others related to you? If so, please explain.

4. Have you ever moved toward others in relationship only to realize that others are not ready to do the same? If so, explain.

5. Have you ever resented someone who put a lot of demand on you or found yourself wanting more time with someone than they are able to give with their busy schedule? If so, please explain.

6. Do you have people in your life who constantly try to recruit you into their busyness? If so, who are they?

7. Have you ever been asked to help someone and you find yourself alone doing their work while they have fun and chat it up with others? If so, who are they?

8. Do you feel that the people in your life genuinely enjoy spending time with you or only use you as a resource? If so, who are they?

9. If you are saying yes to someone in hopes of having a better relationship with them, are your expectations being met or constantly disappointed? If so, please explain.

10. If you find that you give in to certain people or situations over and over again, can you locate why you are doing that? Please explain.

11. Have you ever had someone say no to you? If so, how did you feel?

12. Have you ever decided not to do something that "everyone" else was doing? If so, what was the situation and how did it feel to go against the tide?

13. When you find yourself at odds with the expectations in your

life, do you take the time to examine why you are doing what

you are doing and think about making adjustments?

Notes

Part XI: Finding Your Tribe

Chapter Forty-Two

Who are Your People?

I t's important to locate the people in your life who love and value you throughout all your seasons of life, not just in the ones you share simultaneously. Once you have determined who those people are, hang on to them and cherish them.

When I was young, I moved a lot which meant starting a new school every year. The concept of building lasting connections was foreign to me except in my home and church life.

Every September I was the new person in the class and I began to notice a pattern as the years went by. Girls would gather around me out of friendly curiosity but in time, they would lose interest and go back to their more established friendships. I had little regard for social cliques and wanted to reach out to the people who found themselves alone. It never occurred to me that by doing so I was sealing my own social fate as well.

In high school I did get to attend one school for my secondary education. It was a church school that my parents had started and I was surrounded by church friends. For the first time in my life I felt popular and stable in my friendships.

As life would have it, I went to Bible school far away from the friends I had in that season. When I was finished, my family had moved to a new city where I was starting as the new person once again.

I really think that pattern of temporary connection to friends, combined with my introverted personality and task orientation, impacted how I relate to people to this day.

I've become resistant to meeting new people and investing a lot up front because I see their initial interest as temporary. It's kind of a "you like me now but soon you'll see something about me you don't like and then you'll go back to your old friends" mentality. It takes me a long time to trust and feel safe.

I've also noted that adults are also very cliquey and that by including some people in my life, I've been left off the invite list for certain groups. I've found the unspoken, invisible barriers to be stronger and more unyielding than imaginable.

I can also see where I've behaved and acted in ways to perpetuate my relational dysfunctions. I've even contributed to unspoken, invisible barriers of my own.

All this is to say that when someone did something to hurt me or make me feel unsafe, it was easier for me than most to simply cut them out of my life and not look back. This is the luxury of the young and unwise because as we get older, less and less people are invested in spending the time and energy to reach out to others due to the busyness of their own lives.

If you have someone in your life who cares enough to pick up the phone to call you, take a few minutes to talk to them.

If someone cares enough to extend an invitation to share their life events, and you know they really value your friendship, then do all you can to fit that into your schedule.

If you have someone who thinks you are worth spending their valuable time meeting you for coffee, exercise or some other one-on-one activity, then make the most of it.

Even if you have to withdraw during certain seasons of work and rest, send signals that you miss and value these relationships. Weather the storms. Forgive their shortcomings.

In our "cut those people out of your life" society, work to keep your connections, if even on life support.

One day you may find there are no calls, texts or emails to avoid or invitations to reject. While we can't possibly give all of our time to everyone, find your people who love you enduringly and hang on!

Chapter Forty-Three

Scattering Your Eggs

I t is wise to nurture close relationships but it is also wise to not keep all your eggs in one basket. As wonderful as close relationships are, I've seen them sometimes cloister to the point of being unhealthy and excluding others.

No one person can be all things to us. When I first got married, I wanted my husband to be everything for me: Lover, best friend, provider, parent, buddy etc... I thought marriage meant all we needed was each other. While Shawn is many things to me, he couldn't be all of them at the same time...and he couldn't replace all the roles that other people play in my life.

He couldn't stay up all night playing sleepover girlfriend, whispering secrets and still get up to go to work the next morning. He couldn't fix the car on a Saturday AND go yard saling. He isn't a woman so he couldn't be my best girlfriend and say the words that only another female would know to say.

I learned that I was placing way too much expectation on him for all my happiness and social fulfilment. He's still my favourite human in the whole world but in order for us to preserve our relationship, there has to be space for other people in our lives.

We all have hobbies and interests that are best shared with people who naturally enjoy those same activities. I spent way too much time and energy trying to recruit my husband and friends to do the things I wanted to do but that they had no interest in.

So, scatter your eggs just a little. Join a knitting circle, a book club, a Bible study or a recovery group. Find the common interests between you and your friends and nurture that.

Chapter Forty-Four

Forming New Connections

Stepping back from my job and ministry to rest lead to another difficult and even controversial decision: leaving my church.

I've been raised to "stay where you're planted" so I had been going to the same church for around 30 years when I made this decision. I'm not going to try to justify my decision here in this book except to say that it was completely personal and not a reflection of the church I left. It's a wonderful church filled with amazing leaders and people.

If we were sitting together over coffee, I'd explain all the personal reasons why this decision was another step of bravery and growth for me. Honestly, it would've been easier and much more in my comfort zone to stay where I was. The truth was that I was desperately lonely and unhappy despite my attempts to be involved in serving and leadership and I couldn't quite pinpoint what was wrong.

Now I'm beginning to wonder if it was simply that the church I'd gone to for most of my life was too busy for my personality. It's a large church for Canada and has two Sunday morning services. It was common to meet someone and ask them if they were new only to find out they had been going to the church for many years. You could meet a church acquaintance in a store and ask them where they have been only to find that you've just been going to different services for a long time.

Most people find the buzz of my past home church exciting and love the variety of activities and events. The more I get to know myself, the more I realize that the atmospheric pace stresses me out and doesn't nourish me.

We prayerfully took some time to visit the churches in our city and found one that my husband and I agreed on. We had meaningful conversations with the leadership of the church we were leaving and left with mutual respect. Within a couple weeks of attending our new church we were welcomed into a Life Group that met weekly and they invited us to sit with them on Sunday mornings. This was exactly the welcome I needed.

As months went on, I realized that the single service also contributed to my sense of calm. There was a clear start and end time for everyone so it didn't feel like overlapping shifts. These were just a couple of the things that made me feel a renewed sense of peace and nourishment from my worship experience.

I mention this because leaving a community of people I had shared life with for 30 years was yet another huge challenge for my relationships. In addition to having my spiritual motives questioned, there was the very real obstacle of making new relationships and keeping old ones.

What I learned was encouraging. My close friends stayed with me by meeting me socially for dinner, coffee or exercise dates. Even though our relationship had initially formed at church, my actual interactions with them had flourished outside church for a very long time leading up to this change.

My acquaintances stayed that way on Facebook. I didn't

experience any difference at all. Maybe that is why I was able to make the change in the first place.

Making new friends takes time so it's too soon at the time of this writing to give a fair assessment of how this is going. Our Life Group is very welcoming and personable and I am meeting wonderful new people all the time at the church events we are attending.

The growth and strength in me, due to this realization of my needs and taking action, is huge.

I still think church participation should be long term and committed so I'm not advocating just leaving one's church willy-nilly. It's just that that doesn't it mean you are stuck forever and ever with no regard to your spiritual and relational needs or seasonal life changes.

If you are managing your offences, bringing your gifts to the table, and giving necessary time but you can't shake the need to move on, it's better to prayerfully find a new church that feels like home. No one should bring their body to church without their heart.

Chapter Forty-Five

Connection

One of the best parts of this season of rest is my ability to spend time with the many people I care about. Not just breeze in and out of casual conversation but to have long, heart-to-heart talks. Since I am otherwise at home with complete focus on my writing and household tasks, I don't feel as compelled to check my phone during the visits. I've even left it behind when going for walks. Gasp. I know! It's not an effort, I know those inferior channels of communication will be waiting for me after my visit is complete. I'm less afraid of missing a call, text or message.

At the same time, I observe that my working friends arrive with apologies and check their phones a lot. To the point of distraction. Fortunately for them I have increased my water intake and have to use the bathroom a lot so they can sneak in a call or text without recrimination from me. I remember being as tethered as they are and I don't want to return to that. If anything, I want to be even less tethered.

When someone is with me, I want them to know they have my attention and that I am delighted to be spending time with them. I want to hear their words and share mine. When we say goodbye, I want them to feel like they enjoyed our time together and look forward to a repeat.

I want emotional equity.

For some, this isn't an issue but for me, tight schedules and short visits mean that I never fully relax and feel safe to share my heart or to fully hear my friends' stories. In the time it takes to get past small talk and begin on the deep marrow of heart conversation, the minutes are often cut short too soon.

The paradox is that I'm home alone more this year than in the time I was working and yet I feel more connected. Quality time is my main love language so you can imagine how a schedule starved of quality time could leave me starving for love. During this year, I have the opportunity to experience a couple hours of quality time every single day if I wish and a friend is available! We meet either for coffee or exercise and when we meet, I am really with them and them with me. To say that this has been soul filling would be an understatement. Nothing is more alone that being with a number of people and existing with fragmented conversation time that never brings nourishment to your soul.

Do you live in the "we should get together sometime and talk" or "we'll have to pick up this conversation over coffee one day" existence? I did. Those fulfilments were few and far between. By comparison, now my weeks are as full of those connections as I wish.

Do you have a friend who has as unrelenting of a schedule as you do? When you try to schedule a get-together, do you find yourself at odds trying to find those slivers of times that you're mutually available? Well, I still have some time restraints as I attempt to stay in sync with my husband's working schedule but I am so much more available than before. It feels nice to have that flexibility to work around my friend's life demands when I see them struggling to grab some time with me.

I have friends who are only available during the day and others who can only go out at night. In a dance between my husband's day and afternoon shifts, I get adequate time with them all and I absolutely thrive on it. Did I say I wish this year of rest could continue forever? Oh yes, I wish it could!

Contemplation of Part XI

1. Have you located the people who genuinely care about you by initiating relational time in some way? If so, who are they and how do they express that love?

2. Have you ever experienced being welcomed as a new person and then felt like people lost interest in you for one reason or another? If so, please explain.

3. Have you ever welcomed a new person into your life and then lost interest in them for one reason or another? If so, explain.

4. Have you cut people who love you out of your life and then come to realize that it would've been healthier to work out your differences instead? If so, please explain.

5. Do you see yourself being that caring person for someone else who hasn't fully come to realize the value of your love? If so, please explain.

6. If you are unable to be fully available to your close friends during busy seasons of life, how do you send signals that you still value and care for them so you can reconnect later on?

7. Do you have all your relational eggs in one basket or have you developed a varying bouquet of friendships that meet different needs in your life? If so, please explain.

8. Is it possible that you've depended too much on a limited number of individuals to meet all your needs, thus caused undue pressure on those relationships when they couldn't meet your expectations? If so, please explain.

9. Have you found it necessary to make a decision that tested the ability of some friendships to endure? If so, how?

10. Do you feel that your attempts to slow down your life to a more sustainable rhythm of work and rest is hindered by your relationships or helped?

11. If you had more time to rest, do you think your connections with others would be enhanced or jeopardized? Please explain.

12. Have you experienced the paradox of being lonely in a crowd or connected when alone? If so, please explain.

13. Do you feel like your friendships are deepening with shared conversation and experiences or shallow due to conflicting schedules? Please explain.

14. Do you have a friend who is constantly unavailable to you but seems available to others? How does that make you feel?

15. Do you find yourself constantly unavailable to some people and not to others? Why do you think that is? Is it something you want to fix or is it a way to avoid unpleasantness?

Notes

Part XII: Spiritual Perspective

Chapter Forty-Six

A Matter of Faith

Hopefully the Christian faith I love is evident in my writing even though the matters of work and rest are important for those of every belief system. It was not my desire to write a Christian book marketed solely to Christian people. Neither is it my desire to check my faith at the door of my writing in an attempt to sanitize my work of everything that inspires and guides my life in order to appeal to a greater audience. This is also not a sneaky attempt to persuade my unbelieving readers to my point of view. It just is what it is.

Although I have referred to faith, God, and scriptures through the other sections of this book, I wanted to devote an entire section to the discussions of work and rest in Bible scripture. It is entirely up to you whether you want to include this section in your reading or not but I think you will understand why I included them if you do.

The Bible is full of challenges to work and to rest. So much so that I have often wondered if they don't cancel each other out...how can one do both simultaneously? The Bible is a powerful book as you can take the scriptures not only as a way to live out our lives physically, balancing our work and rest, but spiritually and mentally as we learn to rest and trust in spite of adverse circumstances.

The Bible was written to all mankind from all walks of life. It addresses leaders and slaves, the wealthy and the poor, the wise and the foolish and the righteous and wicked. There is acknowledgement that some are powerless to change anything except their mindset; it promises heavenly justice and rest to all who embrace Jesus, the son of God, who came and died for all sinners.

If you have not embraced Jesus, who is the main character of the Bible, you will be able to glean intellectual knowledge and inspiration from these next chapters but not the internal peace and eternal promises that are buried in them. That treasure is for believers and followers only.

If you read and decide that you would like more information on how to unlock the spiritual application of scripture for your life, please feel free to contact me and I would be delighted to get you more information.

I also want to admit right up front that I'm a student, not a master of these passages. I aspire to be the person who can face adversity with as much grace, peace and trust as I feel in good times that are going my way. Instead, I wrestle with my faith, emotions and desires constantly. One minute I lay them at the cross of suffering that Jesus modelled and the other I pick them up and run in an attempt to secure comfort elsewhere.

My journey has been one of not coming to Jesus trying to be perfect and deserving in my own works but as the broken, selfish person that I am that needs His help.

The following scripture studies feature verses from the King James Version. I enjoy the Shakespearean prose of this classic text but if you find yourself struggling to understand the meaning, I encourage you to look up the passages online in a more modern version. My personal favourites are the New Living Translation and The Message.

Chapter Forty-Seven

Lilies of the Field

"Therefore, I say unto you, take no thought for your life,

what ye shall eat, or what ye shall drink; nor yet for your body,

what ye shall put on. Is not the life more than meat,

and the body than raiment?

Behold the fowls of the air: for they sow not, neither do they

reap, nor gather into barns; yet your heavenly Father

feedeth them. Are ye not much better than they?

Which of you by taking thought

can add one cubit unto his stature?

And why take ye thought for raiment? Consider the lilies of the

field, how they grow; they toil not, neither do they spin:

And yet I say unto you, that even Solomon in all his glory

was not arrayed like one of these.

Wherefore, if God so clothe the grass of the field,

which to day is, and to morrow is cast into the oven,

shall he not much more clothe you, O ye of little faith?

Therefore, take no thought, saying, what shall we eat?

or, what shall we drink? or, wherewithal shall we be clothed?

(For after all these things do the Gentiles seek:) for your

heavenly Father knoweth that ye have need of all these things.

But seek ye first the kingdom of God, and his righteousness;

and all these things shall be added unto you.

Take therefore no thought for the morrow:

for the morrow shall take thought for the things of itself.

Sufficient unto the day is the evil thereof."

Matthew 6:25-34 KJV

read this passage and something inside me is both longing and perplexed.

How do I live that life of unconcern?

What does seeking God's kingdom look like in my lifetime?

My experience has been immersed in church and church work and I see a lot of worried people seeking God's kingdom. They run the gamut of every personality type.

The driven type A, perfectionist followers who live lives of busyness to the neglect of themselves and their loved ones. Often so focused on tasks at hand that they run past opportunities for joy and connection. I've lived a lot of my life in this camp.

Then there are the no worries group who are lovely people in every way but they leave a mess of unpaid bills, unfinished tasks, and lack of realistic planning behind them. One who I could be if I blindly followed the call to rest without balance.

The perfect balance seems impossible.

How do I serve God first and not have to worry about the physical things of life like this passage describes? I've seen beautiful little birds laying dead on the ground after flying into a window and my heart hurts to see it. Where was God for that little bird? He wants me to put aside my worries for self-protection and trust Him like this unfortunate creature?

It just feels like too much to take in and the regretful result is that you have a lot of Christian people who are troubled and worried even more because they are trying to live up to ALL the standards.

As a Christian woman I feel the burden to live an exemplary life as a wife, mother, daughter, sister, worker and CHRISTIAN! I feel the need to take care of my body for health, do all the things of life, serve God selflessly, AND try not to look like an unenviable hag in the process!

At the risk of sounding critical, I look at the modern church leaders in my faith and I see less of Mother Theresa's worn looks and more a line up compatible to Hollywood celebrity grooming. There is tremendous pressure to put aside the frumpy Christian stigma and be relevant but that seems contradictory to scriptures admonition.

I also know that good grooming goes a long way and is a form of honour for one's position. I know people who refuse to bathe regularly, wash and style their hair, take care of their body's hygiene needs or dress appropriately. It is not a reflection of

Godly priorities so much as laziness or blatant misuse of time for personal pleasure. Those individuals repel EVERYONE, believers and unbelievers alike except for the few that can look past it all for a short time in order to minister to them and their needs.

I also see people who show no care for what they eat or drink, accepting all the foods that are offered to them without any effort to discriminate in their meal timing or choices. The effects of chronic restaurant and late-night meals showing in their bodies and long-term health.

On the other hand, I have experienced the restrictions and isolation of making health choices that go against the social norms. I've lived on the "do not call list" for those looking to enjoy dessert splurges. Even though I struggle with weight issues, I consciously avoid restaurant eating, huge portions, buffets and late mealtimes as much as possible.

My weight issues stem more from my exasperated seasons of "not caring". When I stop trying to influence the amount of restaurant visits, the restaurant type and menu selections or when I stop trying to plan or record my daily food intake, I quickly find myself gaining and caring very much again when I experience the consequences of poor food choices.

In light of these paradoxes, I find this passage both wonderful and confusing. What does it mean to live this out practically? Is it more a state of mind?

My takeaway has been to do all the things to live a God-focused life to the best of my ability and trust Him with the end result. Everyone navigates this serving and trusting balance a bit differently based on their spiritual gifts, calling, temperament, resources and level of character. At the end of the day all our efforts cannot change that we will one day see death and it's a humbling of our perspective.

In the season of my sabbatical these words of scripture allow me to rest and believe that God is watching over me during a time where I am consciously performing less than is socially normal. I'm nodding to the price I am paying in annual wage to meander in creativity and life enjoyment while placing myself in the care of my creator for my future. Time will come again soon enough for me to pick up my work and resume the balance of life

but until then, I choose to be a Lily of the Field.

1. What do you feel when you read Matthew 6:25-34? Confusion?

   Relief? Comfort? Troubled? Please explain.

2. What challenges or conflicts do you face in trying to obey this

   passage in modern life?

3. Have you ever felt like you were carrying more pressure as a

   Christian instead of less? Why or why not?

4. What does this passage relay about God's heart and intention

   for our existence?

Chapter Forty-Eight

Rest in the Valley

"The Lord is my shepherd; I shall not want.

He maketh me to lie down in green pastures:

He leadeth me beside the still waters.

He restoreth my soul: He leadeth me in the paths of

righteousness for His name's sake.

Yea, though I walk through the valley of the shadow of death, I

will fear no evil: for thou art with me;

thy rod and thy staff they comfort me.

Thou preparest a table before me in the presence of mine

enemies: thou anointest my head with oil; my cup runneth over.

Surely goodness and mercy shall follow me all the days of my

life: and I will dwell in the house of the Lord for ever."

Psalms 23:1-6 KJV

This is a classic passage of scripture that promises provision, rest, leadership, protection and larger purpose. All the promises hinge on accepting, following and trusting the Lord as a shepherd (caring leader) in our role as part of His flock (cared for follower).

In my years of Christian living somehow my following of Jesus became more fear and performance-based than love and trust-based. Even though I believed I was saved by the grace of Jesus' sacrifice on the cross, I lived a very "if I do this, I'm blessed and if I do that, I'm cursed" existence. I had a difficult time elevating myself out of living solely by the "reap what you sow" mindset. There is a place for this pragmatic logic so I'm not discounting it altogether. It's just that I observed myself and others making mistakes and there was a sense of foreboding in the inevitable "get what we deserved" thinking that made me feel unworthy, less than, and "holding my breath for the shoe to drop". Living purely in the "works" realm of the Christian faith is not life-giving. It kept me in judgement-mode all the time toward myself and others. When I did things well, I looked for my reward. When

I made mistakes, I waited for my punishment. I got angry when others made mistakes and moved toward disaster but even more if it looked like they were "getting away with it".

It really wasn't until I went through a significant trial where I found myself suffering both in my external circumstances and my internal belief system that I realized I was living a life of fear, religion, judgement, endless work and limitations. I felt I had played by "the rules" but clearly not well enough by the results I was getting. I was broken and desolate. That is when I realized my need to truly rest and that, in so doing, I was going to need to depend entirely on God's grace as spoken in the above passage.

The very night after I had made my dramatic decision to quit my job and observe a year sabbatical, I woke completely petrified. What if a disaster struck us because I was perhaps moving out of God's will for my life? Our house could burn down or my family could die. My heart raced as I thought of all the ways I could be opening myself to judgement and consequences. The fear was palpable and I thought about retracting my resignation.

Then I asked myself, "Is that the God that I serve?"

Yes, there are times where God has poured out His judgement for evil deeds in the Bible but would He punish a weary, broken, daughter for claiming rest that He Himself had ordained as holy in the scriptures?

A calm came over me and I felt this passage come alive for me in a way it never had before. It was like a personal promise just for me. For this year, I would abide in my Shepherd's love, provision, protection and rest without fear. I felt as though a circle of protection was enveloping me and all the fear melted away. My entire mind and body relaxed. I knew at that moment everything was going to be okay. Disaster and judgement were not forthcoming because I was being clothed in grace.

This year became a special time for me to know that I have a God that loves me with the tenderness of a Father. He doesn't drive me to perform, work, suppress my emotions, and keep moving on when I need healing and mending. If I was moving in the wrong direction, then I trusted Him to gently re-route me back into His will. My God is bigger than mistakes I make in life course.

The dance between work and rest mirrors the stepping between judgement and grace. While we are invited to come to God in our sin and brokenness, there is an expectation of maturity for those who have lived as Christ-followers for any length of time. It's just that our maturity and growth never cause us to outgrow the need for our Lord's grace and care as a sheep in His flock.

It could be that you've forgotten what it is to be a sheep because you feel like you are acting in the role of shepherd over His flock now. Don't ever forget that you are first a sheep who needs a master's care. Only then can you be a caring shepherd for others.

1. What do you feel when you read Psalm 23:1-6? Please explain.

2. Have you ever experienced God's love, provision, protection and rest? If so, please explain.

3. If you oversee others as a shepherd, do you recognize your own need to be shepherded? If so, how do you stop to get ministered to?

Chapter Forty-Nine

Rest Leads to Rest

"*Let us therefore fear, lest, a promise being left us of entering*

into his rest, any of you should seem to come short of it.

For unto us was the gospel preached, as well as unto them:

but the word preached did not profit them,

not being mixed with faith in them that heard it.

For we which have believed do enter into rest, as He said, as I

have sworn in my wrath, if they shall enter into my rest:

although the works were finished from

the foundation of the world.

For He spake in a certain place of the seventh day on this wise,

and God did rest the seventh day from all His works.

And in this place again, if they shall enter into my rest.

Seeing therefore it remaineth that some must enter therein, and they to whom it was first preached entered not in because

of unbelief: Again, He limiteth a certain day, saying in David,

today, after so long a time; as it is said,

today if ye will hear His voice, harden not your hearts.

For if Jesus had given them rest,

then would He not afterward have spoken of another day.

There remaineth therefore a rest to the people of God.

For he that is entered into his rest,

He also hath ceased from his own works, as God did from His.

Let us labour therefore to enter into that rest,

lest any man fall after the same example of unbelief.

For the word of God is quick, and powerful, and sharper

than any two-edged sword, piercing even to the dividing

asunder of soul and spirit, and of the joints and marrow,

and is a discerner of the thoughts and intents of the heart."

Hebrews 4:1-12 KJV

This passage sounds like a tongue twister of rest that bounces between past, present and future.

Remember in my opening chapters where I correlated our practise of rest on Earth with the promise of heavenly rest? This would be the scriptural basis for that belief.

Nothing is wasted in the Bible. The Genesis account of God creating the world and taking a rest on the seventh day wasn't just a nice story. It also wasn't just the foundation for our present measurement of time — what constitutes a day and a week. It wasn't just an illustration of how God wanted us to practise work and rest on Earth during our lifetimes.

It is all those things and, yet, it is also a promise from the very beginning of time that we will receive heavenly rest in the future. It is tying the obedience of taking rest here on Earth to being given heavenly rest in the future!

How odd that it speaks nothing of work being the qualifier! How much of my life did I see my spiritual service in terms of work and productivity but never rest? Of course, work is implied and exemplified. There is no punctuation of rest without the sentence of work.

This passage also refers to the Old Testament failure of God's chosen people, the Israelites, to successfully enter the rhythm of rest that was required of them. It points to the New Testament fulfilment of Jesus that gives all of us, Jews and Gentiles alike, the opportunity to succeed where our predecessors have failed.

Yet are we any better? How diligent are we to the balance of work and true rest? How many of us truly trust God enough to set down our labour and observe worshipful rest?

The final verse is a powerful one.

"For the word of God is quick, and powerful, and sharper than any two-edged sword, piercing even to the dividing asunder of soul and spirit, and of the joints and marrow, and is a discerner of the thoughts and intents of the heart."

I've previously heard it only as an admonition to read my Bible because it has so much power to transform, which it truly does. However, when I read this passage in a context focused on rest it takes a slightly altered perspective.

The word of God is alive and powerful and, in this passage, He is emphasizing a call to earthly rest and its positioning to heavenly rest. Could it be that the kind of work that we do and how we do it matters? Could it be that the ratio of work we do to the amount of rest we take matters? Could it be that the trust and faith we exhibit when we step away from our labours is as pleasing to God as the diligence with which we actively serve Him in work? Could it be that taking God up in His call to rest better prepares and qualifies us for the Heavenly rest in our futures?

Could it be that as we prayerfully apply this rhythm of work and rest in our lives that it literally sifts our motives and desires and makes them visible to all?

1. What do you feel when you read Hebrews 4:1-13? Please explain.

2. Have you ever contemplated that God values your ability to rest in Him as much as your service to Him?

3. How do you practise your observance of rest? If you don't, why not?

4. What fears, motives and desires become visible to you in your balance of work and rest according to scripture?

Chapter Fifty

Warning to the Lazy

"Go to the ant, thou sluggard; consider her ways, and be wise:

Which having no guide, overseer, or ruler,

provideth her meat in the summer,

and gathereth her food in the harvest.

How long wilt thou sleep, O sluggard?

When wilt thou arise out of thy sleep?

Yet a little sleep, a little slumber,

a little folding of the hands to sleep:

So shall thy poverty come as one that travelleth,

and thy want as an armed man."

Proverbs 6:6-11 KJV

"I went by the field of the slothful,

and by the vineyard of the man void of understanding;

And, lo, it was all grown over with thorns,

and nettles had covered the face thereof,

and the stone wall thereof was broken down.

Then I saw, and considered it well:

I looked upon it, and received instruction.

Yet a little sleep, a little slumber,

a little folding of the hands to sleep:

So shall thy poverty come as one that travelleth;

and thy want as an armed man."

Proverbs 24:30-34 KJV

This is the Puritan call to work that I embraced. It is the ancient wisdom that extols the value of action and productive labour. Laziness is something to be dreaded. Nothing is more disheartening than people who cannot be bothered to provide for themselves or their families. There are many able-bodied people who refuse to work, not for rest but for a lifetime and that is wrong.

This book is not a call to laziness for those who do not wish to work. It is a call to measured rest for those who have laboured too hard and for too long.

My name is Melissa and when I look up the definition of my name, it means "Honeybee" or "Industrious One". I would have preferred "Beautiful One" or "Songbird" but when I look at my life and behaviours, Melissa is a fitting name to describe me.

When I read these scriptures, I feel a low-grade anxiety to move, go, work, and diminish rest. I am particularly sensitive to calls of action. I hear, "Work harder Melissa, because you never know when something bad is going to happen and only your work efforts are going to serve you!"

You can imagine how I have trouble reconciling this passage with Jesus' teachings on not worrying about our lives and His call to lay down our burdens! Sometimes, I had to lay my Bible down because the paradoxes confused and troubled me.

So, I worked to the point of isolation, hoping to perform and please God and man. I grabbed rest guiltily when I was too tired to work always fearing that what I had done wasn't enough.

I am learning that the Bible is indeed powerful in its admonitions and revelations but our reading of it is often clouded by many things. We can read ourselves into passages that aren't addressing us. We can filter through teachings of man, our life views, and our own insecurities. We can read out of context.

If you are like me and you read these words with a sense of stress, then we need to talk. These words are a whip meant for the back of those who refuse to work and support themselves; those who let everything go to waste around them and squander the seasons of their life with zero (I mean zero) regard for their futures.

This is not for people who get up everyday to take care of the business of life and observe the Godly reprieve of rest in appropriate amounts. This is not for those who lay down one form of work to pursue another more meaningful job.

So, my hard-working friends who squander their God-given moments of rest with worries and guilt, you need to put these verses aside and dwell on Jesus' call to rest. Afterward, you can pick up these passages as a reminder to not idle in rest longer than is appropriate.

1. What do you feel when you read the above passages from Proverbs? Please explain

2. Do you know anyone who is suffering the consequences of laziness? If so, who?

3. Do you ever feel "safe" enough to rest? Knowing that you have done "enough" to deserve rest and that disaster will not strike if you do? Please explain.

4. Do you think you live a proper balance of diligence to your affairs and relaxation borne out of trust of God's provision and protection? Please explain.

Chapter Fifty-One

Righteousness Brings Rest and Abundance

"Then judgment shall dwell in the wilderness,

and righteousness remain in the fruitful field.

And the work of righteousness shall be peace; and the effect of

righteousness quietness and assurance for ever.

And my people shall dwell in a peaceable habitation, and in

sure dwellings, and in quiet resting places;

When it shall hail, coming down on the forest;

and the city shall be low in a low place.

Blessed are ye that sow beside all waters,

that send forth thither the feet of the ox and the ass."

Isaiah 32:16-20 KJV

Have you ever watched a talk show or television program with a bunch of lawless drama and wondered at the chaos that sin and wickedness creates? On the other hand, have you seen a program or real-life example where people adhere to Godly living and it brings serene harmony in community?

I was at a family gathering and was drawn into a dramatic conversation by a couple who were not relatives. They were animatedly describing in colourful language an altercation that they had with some friends of theirs. The story was fascinating as they vividly described the drama from their perspective. Not knowing them well enough to have any perspective of my own, I shrugged and commented on the crazy antics they were describing:

"Do your friends have a job? It seems to me that people who don't work have too much time on their hands and create a lot of drama."

I can't remember what they said of the couple in question but there was an awkward silence for a moment and then it came out that the person relaying the story themselves did not currently have a job! Oops! I tried. I still laugh a little when I think of that crazy story and how I put my foot in it trying to empathize with the story tellers!

More than just using busyness to keep out of trouble, it's important to have a *life focus* that keeps us out of trouble. When we are working and resting with a correct *life focus*, then we avoid a lot of the mischief and drama that ruins lives.

This passage equates rest with righteousness. It promises that if people live rightly in obedience to God that He will bless them with safety, rest and home.

Even if there is turmoil all around there will be blessing in their work as they continue on.

What a remarkable reminder that obedience to God is rewarded with security, work fruitfulness and rest!

1. What do you feel when you read the above passages from Isaiah 32:16-20? Please explain.

2. Have you ever witnessed "unrighteous" people stir up drama and create a lot of turmoil for themselves and others? If so, please explain.

3. Have you ever witnessed "righteous" people who live serenely, beautiful lives that are a blessing to themselves and others? Please explain.

4. Do you see chaos in your own life that could be replaced with peace if you submitted an area of disobedience to God? If so, please explain.

Chapter Fifty-Two

Lay Down Your Burden

"Come unto me, all ye that labour and are heavy laden,

and I will give you rest.

Take my yoke upon you, and learn of me;

for I am meek and lowly in heart:

and ye shall find rest unto your souls.

For my yoke is easy, and my burden is light."

Matthew 11:28-30 KJV

I have read this scripture many times wondering about how tired I feel and how heavy my burdens are. Where is the rest? Why does my Christian experience feel like an endless treadmill of services, meetings, practises, activities and volunteerism?

I remember at one point when my children were in grade school we were going to church, hosting a mentor group, attending a mentor's group and taking weekly leadership trainings with weekend spiritual retreats four times a year! This didn't include the few hours every month of volunteering during services.

This was all in addition to work, home care and child rearing responsibilities and we were grasping at how to do it all well. Fortunately, there were some much needed changes in what the church was doing to make their programs more sustainable for families long term. There was good intention behind it and we laugh about the craziness now but it was also an important reminder of how easily we can get caught up in group programs.

While I definitely kept out of trouble due to the amount of activity we were involved in during that season, we could have gotten into trouble if we'd lived life at that speed without adjusting our course.

I'm not against church programs. I've been helped by them and I've led them to help others. It's just that it's easy to see our service and ability to help others solely in that context and we can get caught up in a clinical, formula approach to Christian life instead of a naturally-occurring one.

I remember thinking that in all my busy Christian activities, I had zero relationship with my actual neighbours! In fact, I was so immersed in Christian life that I rarely came across non-Christian people at all except in very brief encounters in the marketplace.

It wasn't that the church work I was doing was wrong or bad and that it wasn't helping those that other people brought to church...it's just that something about how I was racing through life past natural relationship opportunities felt off.

When I did slow down, I realized that I found it difficult to change. I had gotten so used to building relationships in the structure of the church that I didn't know how to progress them in a neighbourly context. I've been walking my dogs around the neighbourhood and am slowly getting comfortable with stopping to chat with neighbours we happen upon. Not in a grasp to convert and invite to church but solely just to be neighbourly and social.

This may sound elementary to many but we were *that* busy and when we were not working, we found it easier to zone out with television or reading than extend ourselves outside our home to people who weren't involved in our "world".

So, part of taking an easier yoke and lighter burden is to minimize the text of my life and increase the margin and spacing so that there is room for the unexpected "between the lines" to occur naturally.

I'm also not as gifted verbally as I am in my writing. Sometimes, I would get discouraged because I feel very inept to speak the faith I hold in casual conversation. I can teach a class or write a blog post but a verbal interaction feels harder for some reason. Part of finding an easier yoke and lighter burden is to accept my limitations and embrace my gifts. Maybe there is less responsibility to be verbally adept and more to simply express myself in the way God made me strong.

Another way we can lay down our burdens is to consider putting down some of the things we prize in submission to God's call. Never underestimate the power of relinquishing our will. If you've been feeling a deep call to put aside something you feel is important and you've been fighting to hold on, you will experience instant rest and peace when you finally decide to let it go. It may be that you find it given back to you later but it won't have the hold on your affections that it once did.

If you feel like your life is heavy and burdensome, please take some time to contemplate why. If you are not a believer, you may find rest by simply deciding to no longer live life on your own terms. If you are a believer who has forgotten your first love and now feels caught on an endless treadmill of good activities...you may need to take a break, reconnect and recalibrate your life.

1. What do you feel when you read the above passages from Matthew 11:28-30? Please explain.

2. Have you ever felt that following Jesus was a wearying, heavy burden to carry? If so, why do you think that is?

3. Have you found rest for your soul as a Christian? If not, why do you think that is?

4. Jesus is communicating comfort and love as a teacher for His apprentices (us). Have you experienced that? Why or why not?

5. Can you locate something that you have not let go of (habit, mindset etc.) that is keeping you from embracing Jesus' call to lay down your burden and accept His?

Chapter Fifty-Three

The Fourth Commandment

Part V "The Lost Art of Rest" contained a chapter named "Weekly Rest" that talks about observing the Bible's Sabbath. Still, the Bible has so much to say about setting apart a day every week for worship and rest that I wanted to go into more detail in this section that focuses on spiritual perspective.

Sabbath rest seemed incredibly important to God. Even though this command was given to the Israelites in the Old Testament (covenant) and most of us are Gentiles living by the New Testament (covenant), this importance is plain to see.

First, God himself modelled this behaviour by working six days and resting on the seventh in the second chapter of the Bible:

"Thus, the heavens and the earth were finished,

and all the host of them.

And on the seventh day God ended His work

which He had made; and He rested on the seventh day from all

His work which He had made.

And God blessed the seventh day, and sanctified it:

because that in it He had rested from all his work

which God created and made."

Genesis 2:1-3 KJV

Later, God included the observation of rest in the infamous Ten Commandments. Right in there with abstaining from lying, stealing, murdering and committing adultery!

Over and over again the Israelites were instructed to keep this commandment to rest once a week even under the penalty of death and they still found it difficult to obey! It is important to remember that issuing a death penalty for violating community "rules" was very commonplace in this time of history. Disobedience of established authority was taken more seriously than it is today. It's not so much the significance of the sin that was committed as the significance of the One the sin was committed against. When we remember who God is and the significance of His commands, the severity of disobedience takes on greater context.

"And the Lord spake unto Moses, saying,

Speak thou also unto the children of Israel, saying, verily my

Sabbaths ye shall keep: for it is a sign between me and you

throughout your generations; that ye may know that

I am the Lord that doth sanctify you.

Ye shall keep the Sabbath therefore; for it is holy unto you:

every one that defileth it shall surely be put to death: for

whosoever doeth any work therein,

that soul shall be cut off from among his people.

Six days may work be done; but in the seventh is the Sabbath

of rest, holy to the Lord: whosoever doeth any work in the

Sabbath day, he shall surely be put to death.

Wherefore the children of Israel shall keep the Sabbath,

to observe the Sabbath throughout their generations,

for a perpetual covenant.

It is a sign between me and the children of Israel for ever:

for in six days the Lord made heaven and earth,

and on the seventh day he rested, and was refreshed.

And He gave unto Moses, when He had made an end of

communing with him upon mount Sinai, two tables of testimony,

tables of stone, written with the finger of God."

Exodus 31:12-18 KJV

Obedience came with promises, not only for the children of Israel, but for foreigners and eunuchs who committed themselves to following the Jewish faith.

"Blessed is the man that doeth this, and the son of man that

layeth hold on it; that keepeth the Sabbath from polluting it,

and keepeth his hand from doing any evil.

Neither let the son of the stranger, that hath joined himself to

the Lord, speak, saying, The Lord hath utterly

separated me from his people:

neither let the eunuch say, Behold, I am a dry tree.

For thus saith the Lord unto the eunuchs that keep my

Sabbaths, and choose the things that please me,

and take hold of my covenant;

Even unto them will I give in mine house and within my walls a

place and a name better than of sons and of daughters:

I will give them an everlasting name, that shall not be cut off.

Also, the sons of the stranger, that join themselves to the Lord,

to serve Him, and to love the name of the Lord, to be his

servants, every one that keepeth the Sabbath from polluting it,

and taketh hold of my covenant;

Even them will I bring to my holy mountain, and make them

joyful in my house of prayer: their burnt offerings and their

sacrifices shall be accepted upon mine altar; for mine house

shall be called a house of prayer for all people."

Isaiah 56:2-7 KJV

"If thou turn away thy foot from the Sabbath,

from doing thy pleasure on my holy day;

and call the Sabbath a delight, the holy of the Lord,

honourable; and shalt honour Him, not doing thine own ways,

nor finding thine own pleasure, nor speaking thine own words:"

Isaiah 58:13 KJV

God took the observance of rest very personally and was frustrated that His children insisted on living life and working on their own terms. Rest was a blessing and meant to refresh His people. God made promises of blessing and fruitfulness to those who obeyed. Still, there was human resistance to this mandate.

In addition, it seems that some observed the tradition but without the spirit of love that inspired it. Jesus challenges the Pharisees in the New Testament by breaching their definition of Sabbath observance. This angered the Pharisees who purposed to live out the law with frustration and anger toward those who didn't.

"And it came to pass, that He went through the corn fields

on the Sabbath day; and His disciples began,

as they went, to pluck the ears of corn.

And the Pharisees said unto Him, behold,

why do they on the Sabbath day that which is not lawful?

And He said unto them, have ye never read what David did,

when he had need, and was an hungred,

he, and they that were with him?

How he went into the house of God in the days of Abiathar the

high priest, and did eat the shewbread, which is not lawful to eat

but for the priests, and gave also to them which were with him?

And He said unto them, the Sabbath was made for man,

and not man for the Sabbath:

Therefore, the Son of man is Lord also of the Sabbath."

Mark 2:23-28 KJV

Jesus didn't say there is no need to observe the Sabbath so lets just forget all about it from now on. He adjusted the heart with which the Sabbath was supposed to be taken.

The Sabbath is meant to meet the needs of people, not crush them!

My journey has highlighted the importance of the Sabbath in my life but not in a religious requirement that makes me more worthy of God's love. No! Taking a day out from my week to go to church, rest, connect with family and other believers is a gift to myself and God.

If I feel that pressure bearing down on me and isolating me from joy and other people then I adjust to make room for love, warmth and refreshment.

I must warn you that some Christians believe we need to be dogmatic in following the mosaic law's observance to the detail. It's important to remember that we are not Old Testament Jews. We are New Testament Gentiles. The debate about what was expected from New Testament Gentiles in terms of mosaic law observance was settled early on in the New Testament.

Jesus, Himself, elevated everyone from justification by following the mosaic law for redemption of sin to being justified by grace. Jesus elevated the commandments to acts of love that we offer God in spirit and in truth.

Some would say we need to practise worship and sabbath rest on Saturday like the Jews do instead of Sunday like most Christian faiths do. I don't believe God is as concerned with the chosen day so much as that you are showing your love and trust in Him on one designated day each week. A day where you can connect with your faith community, family and take a rest from work activities.

If you are challenged and confused by this in our seven day, 24-hour world, I'm not surprised. I would advise you to pray and ask God what sabbath rest should look like for you and adjust as you are able.

Going to a weekly church service is a good start. Maybe planning your week so you can have that day off work is another. If you can, get your household chores and errands done outside that day. Try planning ahead so you don't need to go to the market or eat at a restaurant which causes others to work.

Whatever your effort, let it come from a place of honour and love for God, yourself and others.

It is not a competition. There is no award for best Sabbath keeper. Most of the rewards will be intangible but watch and see if you do not experience God in a fuller way than ever before as a result.

More scriptures on sabbath rest: Exodus 20:8-11, Exodus 34:21, Exodus 35:1-3, Leviticus 16:31, Leviticus 19:3, Leviticus 19:30, Leviticus 23:32, Leviticus 26:2, Deuteronomy 5:12-15, 2 Chronicles 36:21, Ezekiel 22:8

1. What do you feel when you read the many passages about keeping the Sabbath? Please explain.

2. The observance of weekly rest seemed very important to God in the Old Testament, why do you think that was?

3. There are no clear instructions to observe the Sabbath in the New Testament for the Christian church or for Gentiles but do you think that weekly rest is any less important to God today? Why or why not?

4. If you were to begin incorporating weekly rest in your life in a love and worshipful expression of your faith, what would that look like?

Chapter Fifty-Four

Rhythm of Planting and Rest

I covered this scripture in detail in the earlier section called "The Lost Art of Rest," but it is worth repeating.

"And six years thou shalt sow thy land,

and shalt gather in the fruits thereof:

But the seventh year thou shalt let it rest and lie still;

that the poor of thy people may eat: and what they leave the

beasts of the field shall eat. In like manner thou shalt deal with

thy vineyard, and with thy oliveyard.

Six days thou shalt do thy work, and on the seventh day thou

shalt rest: that thine ox and thine ass may rest, and the son of

thy handmaid, and the stranger, may be refreshed."

Exodus 23:10-12 KJV

On a recent trip to Israel I got to see first hand how the Orthodox Jews practise the seven-day rest in Jerusalem. The hotel we stayed at became more populated with local families and we were told that many come to stay at hotels for the Sabbath. There was a designated elevator that stopped at every floor automatically so no one would have to push a button. The buffet quality was less because staffing was lower and it seemed as though some of the food had been reheated from the day before. The city of Jerusalem slowed down.

For us looking in as tourists this interruption to goods and services was a bit of a "Oh yeah" moment. It was both beautiful and bothersome. On one hand it was interesting and wondrous that the Orthodox were paying tribute to their cultural roots and religious beliefs. Something unique and reverent in our modern times. On the other hand, it was inconvenient and bothersome and even a bit ridiculous in its practise with opting for a hotel visit rather than preparing one's home or the automatic elevator stops.

Most importantly it made me think about the beliefs I have and how I practise them. The spirit of those beliefs and the contradictions of my practise to those outside looking in on my life like tourists.

I don't know any culture that embraces the seven-year rest. A year is a long time to cease one's work and our modern society races forward. Who would dare to close shop for so long?

1. What do you feel when you read the passage in Exodus 23:10-12? Please explain.

2. If you lived in the time of this commandment as part of the Israeli people, what do you think the obstacles would be to keeping this observance?

3. Why do you think this commandment was given by God? Do you see it as a control and a test or an expression of love for His people? Why?

4. What do you think about modern day observances of this rest principle, not as a religious mandate but personal love and worshipful expression?

5. Since this book focuses on the therapeutic and growth benefit of taking a sabbatical, have you taken an interest in the idea of completing one yourself? Please explain?

Chapter Fifty-Five

Futility of Work Without God

"Except the Lord build the house, they labour in vain that build

it: except the Lord keep the city,

the watchman waketh but in vain.

It is vain for you to rise up early, to sit up late, to eat the bread

of sorrows: for so he giveth his beloved sleep."

Psalms 127:1-2 KJV

Have you ever worked really hard for something that ended up being a waste? Either your work was destroyed or it was rejected? It can be so demoralizing when our toil is unproductive or misdirected.

This passage talks about the futility of work by those who are in opposition to God and His purposes. At the same time, it talks about rest that is given to those who are aligned with Him and His purposes.

1. What do you feel when you read the passage in Psalm 127:1-2? Please explain.

2. Have you ever invested yourself into work that proved futile? If so, how did that feel?

3. Do you see the value of taking time for God and for rest as a balance to devoting all your life to work in an effort to "save yourself"? Please explain.

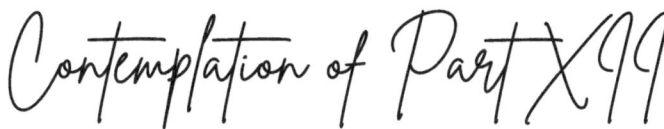

Contemplation of Part XIV

1. Were you aware that so many scriptures in the Bible refer to the importance of rest?

2. Has the study of these scriptures impacted your perspective of rest as part of Christian worship?

3. How are you planning to add rest to your life in the future and how will that increase your reliance on God?

Notes

Part XIII: Setting Intentions

Chapter Fifty-Six

Geocaching

O n a past weekend camping trip we decided to make a game of geocaching. Boys against girls. I pulled out my long unused app to spot the nearby caches. There was only one "free" cache within proximity to our campground but there were many more all around us if we were willing to upgrade the app for $8.50. In light of my recent lifestyle changes, I subdued my knee jerk reaction of just paying for convenience so we opted for "free".

The search and find of the free geocache sparked some interest in our young campers so we decided to go in search of another free geocache that was over 1km away. Very quickly, we had campers who lost interest but there were a few of us who were doggedly determined to see this through until the end.

I had an idea that the search was going to take us into an adjoining park and all we had to do was follow the beaten path for the 1km to find it. At some point though, we realized that the number of metres was increasing, not decreasing and that the geocache app was showing we were walking away from our target. How could this be? It took some time but we realized that the geocache had been 1km from our original location "across a huge separating ravine" and that our path would take us there but in a very, long roundabout way that would take three times as long if not more. By the time we realized what was going on, it was a toss up as to whether we should turn back by foot to our campsite or just proceed to the nearest pickup point at the visitor centre of the other park and have one of our campers drive over to rescue us. We ended up moving forward, abandoning our cache search and getting picked up at the visitor centre of the remote park. It had turned into a 3-hour hike.

Pondering this later, I mused how like real life this incident had been. Isn't it common to seek after a goal, thinking it is a straightforward distance away only to find that our path takes many unexpected twists and turns, sometimes leading us away from what we want and sometimes we abandon what we started out wanting for a new destination? Our final destination wasn't intended at all but rather the result of a journey started for a completely different purpose which went unexpectedly awry.

I was also experiencing some delayed anger at the event. Why hadn't I just paid the $8.50 for the more readily accessible geocaches? Why didn't the geocache app show the map area better so I could've better assessed our goal? What if we hadn't had the option of a ride back to the campground? We didn't even accomplish what we set out to do! This frustration and annoyance mirrored some of my thoughts about my own life goals and accomplishments. Where I had set my course was not where I had landed at all. I felt angry at not better knowing the path I was setting on. Choices I had made or not made that could've help me make better decisions earlier.

In the end we had an adventure and our young adventurers were enthusiastic despite the turn of events. No-one got hurt. We found our way. We had a ride back to the campground and a prepared meal when we arrived. We were okay. We had gotten more exercise than we bargained for. Life happened and we had prevailed with a little help even if we didn't do what we set out to do.

Chapter Fifty-Seven

Setting Goals

Just like the misadventure while geocaching, we must be prepared that even our best plans may take us on unexpected adventures.

When I decided to take a year off of working to rest and replenish, I didn't know where that decision would take me. It was like stepping off a cliff. That's probably why I waited until I was almost delirious with exhaustion and burnout to take the step.

When I made the decision, I soon found myself asking what I wanted from that year at home. Certainly, I wasn't going to sleep and watch television nonstop. No! I was being given a precious year of discretionary time to do whatever brought my heart joy and rest and there was no guarantee I would get another opportunity like this.

I made a list of things that I wanted to do. Travel was out because we hadn't saved enough for that and Shawn was still working. I was okay with that though because home really was my destination of choice.

I wanted to clean my home from top to bottom, organize the house, do some scrap-booking and organize our computer files and photos. I also wanted to write my first book. It was an ambitious list and a friend jokingly reminded me about not forgetting the "rest" part of my year.

It was good that I made a list of things that I wanted to accomplish and I've worked on a few things being careful not to be driven about it. Cleaning and organizing my house were fun for a month, I haven't gotten to the scrap-booking or the computer tasks but oh, how I have revelled in the joy of writing!

I really had no idea that this journey would lead to me starting a blog in addition to working on this book. Before this year I never referred to myself as a writer but now I do. It's not about skill or success, it's about finally recognizing who I truly am and what brings me joy and fulfilment.

I have five months left of my sabbatical at the time of this writing and I still have no idea what is next. Ideally, my blog and the writing of this book would generate some sustainable income so that I could remain exactly where I am now. I may need to return to a part-time job of some kind. I honestly don't know.

What I do know is that I discovered something precious this year and it has changed my life. I've invested myself into something that has untold potential for the future and nothing will be lost even if I do return to full time work.

I'm glad I set goals at the start but I didn't have the capacity to plan what has unfolded this year in the midst of the journey.

That, my friends, is the definition of adventure!

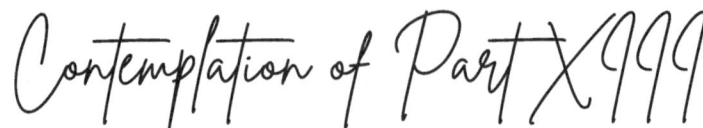

Contemplation of Part XVIII

1. Have you ever set out on a journey only to realize that your destination was not where you thought it was? If so, please explain.

2. Did you ever have to deal with anger toward yourself or others for decisions you made based on information or expectations that were not met? If so, please explain.

3. Have you experienced an adventure that didn't turn out as expected but the result was just as good, if not better? Please explain.

4. Have you made a life altering decision knowing in your heart it was the absolute right thing to do but didn't know where it would lead? If so, please explain.

5. What are your goals and how are you going to move toward them?

Notes

Part XIV: Let Transformation Begin

Chapter Fifty-Eight

Keeping a Journal

As with all great adventures, you must record your journey by keeping a journal. It may surprise you to know that I've never mastered the skill of daily journaling so I had to come up with a different approach. Instead of a daily account, I simply sit down and summarize my activities every month or so.

The cool thing about journaling every month versus every day is that I get a much higher perspective of my journey than if I just focused on each individual day's events. I saw the huge progressions and didn't get caught up in the daily mundane.

I saw myself transform from a hurting, tired, depleted and frustrated person to a healthy, happy, energized and effective one. I saw how one decision, opportunity or experience led to another and another until the life I was living was completely transformed with every event building on the one before it.

With more sabbatical months behind me than before me, it's easy to feel like the time has slipped through my fingers and to panic about the future. When I read my monthly journal entries, I am reminded of how much has transpired and how quickly life can change for the better. It gives me encouragement that my sabbatical story is still not fully told and my destination not yet determined. It's not over until it's over.

So, whether you are a natural writer or not, find some way to memorialize your rest journey and to celebrate where it takes you. Whatever your adventures, I am certain you will look back and see that your life grew exponentially during your season of rest.

When I was pregnant with my children, I was convinced that every minute of much needed sleep was time that my precious baby was growing. I never felt guilty for the naps and long nights sleeps because I knew I was creating life and my body was working hard to expand with it.

Your rest time is the same. You will experience growth that could never happen during your season of work. You need to bask in every minute and not give a moment of time to feeling guilt. You are creating life and expanding. The season of work will come soon enough and when it does, you will be ready to embrace it.

Chapter Fifty-Nine

I am Home

All the sacrifices of material goods, services and being willing to disappoint the expectations of others should lead to a beautiful place that is difficult to express in words that others understand. It is not suffering for suffering's sake. No, it is not a loss but a redistribution of wealth to areas that are less tangible to others but blossom like a garden to you and the ones under your care.

A few months into my sabbatical I reflected on how this year is such a gift. I cannot express how fulfilling it has been to be home full time caring for my family. As I fill my days with the mundane chores of cooking, cleaning, running errands, taking care of my dogs, meeting friends for walks, making meals to be shared with friends, and practising self-care as I rehabilitate from the effects of sustained inactivity...I am overcome with gratitude.

I did not just come home. I AM home. Our house is just an empty shell but when I bring my heart here and fill it with love and care, it becomes home.

My son gave me a card for Valentines Day that spoke this sentiment perfectly. So much so that I took a picture of the script:

My Mother's Heart

There's a beautiful place

I can always call home

It's not a house

I once lived in,

Or a town

I grew up in

But a special place -

A place of hope

And encouragement,

Happiness and love.

When I put my dishes away, I am thanking God that I can put them carefully where they belong.

When I do the laundry, I am overcome by the privilege of being able to fold our clothes and place them in neatly arranged dresser drawers.

When my son needs a ride because the weather is so cold that it's not safe to take the bus, I am relieved that I am free to do this for him.

When my daughter picks up the phone to talk and I can set aside my schedule to listen and advise, I am glad I was there to take the call and linger in it.

I love that I can serve Shawn by doing chores that I am capable of doing so he can focus on what I cannot.

In all this, my heart and mind are constantly wondering about God and His plans and expectations of me. So often it is communicated that serving Him means setting aside this wonderful role to be something more...but what if this is enough? What if me being happy and content just being the heartbeat of my home is all He created me to be and that brings Him pleasure too?

I am home.

Contemplation of Part XLVIV

1. Do you currently keep a regular journal? If not, why?

2. Can you see the value of documenting your progress toward a better work rest balance periodically? If yes, how do you plan to do that?

3. Do you feel any disparity (difference) between other's expectations for your life versus God's as revealed in the Bible and in your heart? If so, please explain.

4. Are you able to accept a life that appears to be less than others if you know that you are being true to what you were created to do? (Living your purpose?)

5. Did you find yourself inspired by some of the thoughts, text and conclusions in this book? How?

6. Do you see yourself making adjustments to your work/rest life rhythm as a result of what you read in this book? If so, how?

7. If you feel drawn to take an extended period of rest, are you prepared to do the research, have the conversations, and make the necessary financial adjustments to ensure you've done your part to be responsible? If yes, please explain.

8. If you are embarking on a long-term season of rest, assuming you have done your part, how are you trusting God to provide for you during your season of rest?

9. Did you become more aware of your Creator and His love and provision for you as part of reading this book? If so, please explain.

Notes

Chapter Sixty

Conclusion

Thank you for taking the time to read about my journey. I hope that you have been inspired to set aside some measure of time for rest of your own. Maybe it will be as subtle as allowing for better sleep or becoming more serious about taking a day of rest in your weekly schedule. Maybe it will be as dramatic as quitting your job and going to an overseas destination for a year-long sabbatical.

Whatever your chosen path, I challenge you to approach it thoughtfully and prayerfully. Think through all the implications and prepare for contingencies. The last thing I would want is to see someone make a life-altering decision without counting the potential cost to themselves and their family.

Having said that, once you've had the conversations and run the numbers and embarked on your personal journey of rest and change, don't look back. Forge forward and live this precious, beautiful long-term event we call life.

Dream your dreams and seize your joy. Give up the trinkets of life to drink deeply of what is truly important and vital to your soul. Who knows? You may transform like a caterpillar to a butterfly and never return to the place you once were.

I would love to hear about your adventures and experiences. Memorialize your journey and celebrate your progress. Then share your story with me. Nothing would give me greater joy than to know my words brought inspiration and motivation to your days that you never thought possible.

Above all, if reading this book led you to an awareness of our Creator...the very author of our world, of us and the concepts of work and rest, please let me know. I truly believe that without God, even an entire year of blissful rest would be meaningless. It is only the Divine's vibrant power of regeneration and refreshment that brings life to the weary soul.

If you enjoyed my writing, please visit www.LeavingBusy.com and subscribe to receive my weekly blog articles. My posts are full of inspirations to help you in your journey to rest and create a sustainable life pace for you and your family.

Swirl Divider used throughout this book was
Designed by Freepi